DOCKERS
THE '95 TO '98 LIVERPOOL LOCKOUT

DAVE SINCLAIR

FOREWORD BY KEN LOACH

AMBERLEY

*This book is dedicated to the Dockers, their wives and families,
and is also in memory of my sister Una Edwards 1961–2015.*

First published 2015

Amberley Publishing
The Hill, Stroud
Gloucestershire, GL5 4EP

www.amberley-books.com

Copyright © Dave Sinclair, 2015

The right of Dave Sinclair to be identified as the Author of this work has been asserted in accordance with the Copyrights, Designs and Patents Act 1988.

ISBN 978 1 4456 4848 4 (print)
ISBN 978 1 4456 4849 1 (ebook)

All rights reserved. No part of this book may be reprinted or reproduced or utilised in any form or by any electronic, mechanical or other means, now known or hereafter invented, including photocopying and recording, or in any information storage or retrieval system, without the permission in writing from the Publishers.

British Library Cataloguing in Publication Data.
A catalogue record for this book is available from the British Library.

Typeset in 11pt on 13pt Celeste.
Typesetting by Amberley Publishing.
Printed in the UK.

FOREWORD BY KEN LOACH

The Liverpool Docks lockout of the 1990s was a decisive moment in our post-war history. What was at stake was the nature of work itself. Was it, as the working class needed, secure jobs with a reliable income, good enough to bring up a family and live a dignified life, or was work to be seen as units of labour, as the employers wanted, to turn on and off like a tap, with no obligation to the workforce beyond paying the least amount possible to them or to the contractors who hired them.

It was the final act in the drama that began in 1979, with the Tory election victory and Thatcher's arrival as Prime Minister. War was waged on organised labour. The withdrawal of government support closed factories, saw unemployment rise to three million and wrecked the social fabric of old industrial communities. Strikes were provoked that established a pattern of victories for the employers and the government that stood behind them. Laws were enacted to weaken the Trades Unions' power to respond quickly and effectively to management attacks.

Then came the miners. The great strike that lasted a year to defend the pits, and thereby jobs and communities, was engineered by Thatcher's government and, despite the heroic efforts of the miners and their families, was lost. The rank and file of the labour movement did all in its power to no avail. The leadership of the Labour Party did not want to inherit a strong union movement if ever they were to get back into power and were content for the Tories to oversee the miners' defeat. Other union leaders were of a similar mind and had watched their own or other unions fall to defend jobs. Why should the miners not suffer a similar fate?

With unions in retreat, the way was clear to transform the relationship between employer and worker in favour of the employer. But no one told the Liverpool Dockers. The writer Jim Allen, manual worker and socialist, once said to me that if there were to be a revolution in England it would start in Liverpool. The Petrograd of England he called it. We had made films together there and his words rang true. The men and women I met were hardened and enlightened by generations of political struggle. It was no surprise that they should resist the attempt to remove their hard-won security.

The dispute began, as so often, with a series of provocations by the employers. Other ports were using non-union casual labour. From the employers' point of view, why should Liverpool be the exception? But who would choose to be a day labourer, never knowing when you would work or not? Dock workers have long memories. The days of struggling in the pen to catch the eye of the man who could hire you or not were vividly remembered. Why should that humiliation be allowed to return?

The dock workers were locked out, agency workers were brought in and the long struggle began. My memories are made vivid by Dave Sinclair's evocative pictures. They are a fine record of that extraordinary effort We were able to make a documentary film which meant we were present at some critical moments.

I remember the weekly meetings, models of democratic engagement – everyone allowed to speak, reports of various activities, arguments made with passion, anger and determination.

I can remember the international solidarity. Dockers from around the world understood the significance of the struggle. There were messages, visits and support action in foreign ports. What power we would have, if only we were properly organised!

I remember the Women of the Waterfront, every bit as formidable in the determination that the dispute should be won as the miners' wives a decade earlier. Who knows what hardships and difficulties families faced behind closed doors, but in public the women were a strong presence, politically sharp and emotionally brave.

There was one occasion when the redoubtable Doreen McNally rounded on Peter Hain, Labour minister at the T.U.C. conference. His pretence of support for the dockers was exposed as empty platitudes by Doreen and the group around her. Bill Morris, General Secretary of the T.G.W.U. suffered similar treatment. Having told the dockers in the early days of the dispute that they would never walk alone, they were abandoned by a union that had no strategy to win. Once again the interests of working-class people were betrayed by the hollow men who claimed to lead them.

Every dispute has its picket lines, its big demonstrations and mass action. There is a familiar pattern: start by fighting the employer, then confront the police, and finally have to battle with the union and labour leaders.

Could the Dockers have won? The tide was against them. The employers had had victory after victory and it would have needed a brilliantly organised campaign of international action to reinstate the dockers in permanent jobs. The potential for victory is always there, but it needs leadership with the same confidence in its class that the employers and the politicians have in theirs.

But the hope that one day we shall get there remains. You only have to look in the eyes of the men and women in Dave Sinclair's photographs to realise it is the only war worth fighting.

DOREEN MCNALLY

Margaret Thatcher came into power with a bucket list: deregulation, privatisation and destruction of the trade unions. She took a sledgehammer to the manufacturing industries and after a year-long, heroic struggle by our miners, they were defeated. As a result, working-class confidence was dented and unions were not fit for purpose. In 1989, against this backdrop, she came for the Dockers.

There was a national dock strike against deregulation and a return to casual labour, but one by one the other ports returned as we watched horrified. Liverpool was left standing alone and the men had no choice but to return. The company embarked on a demoralisation program, and by issuing 'take it or leave it' contracts, they forced many older men to take early retirement.

The same men were expected to be at the end of a phone, 24/7; they would be called at a moment's notice to change shift patterns, intruding on family life to an unacceptable level and causing constant provocation. Young Torside Dockers were unjustly sacked in the port while the rest of the Dockers supported them. The result – the company locked them out and sacked the entire workforce.

Women had never been directly involved in disputes at the port before, so to be asked to attend and speak at a rally clearly illustrated that this was something different. Dockers' Daughters and Dockers' wives, most of whom hadn't met before but all with childhoods steeped in the reality of how hard-earned our social gains were, met in the transport and general workers union offices. A couple of shop stewards answered questions, explaining what they could, and Sylvia Pye from the Miners' Wives spoke to us.

Amid shock and confusion we began the process of organising, learning on our feet. Welfare rights advisors ran a course to give us a basic understanding and remained with us, making an invaluable contribution because, along with everything else, we were confronted with worries over homes, debts and bills. We distributed donated food, sold merchandise, and attended and spoke at conferences and meetings locally, nationally and internationally. We dealt with the media and the inevitabilities of life, celebrating births and hiding grief, afraid of losing our coping mechanism. We politicised our children, propped up our husbands and each other, gave a platform and support to others in struggle and gained a political education that could not be bought or learned from books.

International support was solid, but at home the unions hid behind the anti-trade union laws – a direct contravention of the charter for human rights (Britain is a founding signatory). Meanwhile, New Labour leader Tony Blair was bragging in Hong Kong that we had the most restrictive trade union laws in the world and he had no intention of changing that. Abandoned and betrayed by both the unions and political party, there was nowhere else to go. David Sinclair photographed the dispute from start to finish, telling our story in a way that a library full of words couldn't. He photographed the carnival of the rallies, the elation of the international support and the police. He caught the laughter, tears, hardship and courage, the disappointments, the weariness and the children. His work illustrates the human cost and his evocative and powerful photographs capture our souls.

The Casa on Hope Street Liverpool is a club that was bought by the Dockers with proceeds from the film by Jimmy McGovern, *Dockers*, produced by Sally Hibben. People can go there for help and advice. It is also the home of Unite the Union community 567 Branch, boasting more than 1,000 members. It represents a community working together in an organised, structured way to achieve our bucket list: just one item – social justice.

MIKE CARDEN & JIMMY NOLAN

Dave Sinclair began recording 'images of the Liverpool dock dispute' on Wednesday 27 September 1995. Two days earlier, a small dock labour supply company, Torside Ltd, had dismissed its entire labourforce of eighty young dockers. The majority of these young men were the sons of dockers working for the Port Authority, the Mersey Docks and Harbour Company. The following day, Thursday 28 September 1995, the Torside dockers picketed the gates of the Seaforth Docks. Dockers refused to cross their picket lines and within just a few hours 500 Liverpool dockers had been dismissed.

So began the Liverpool dock dispute, it was not a strike, these men had been all dismissed. Even though they had no employer the official trade union claimed they could not support this 'unofficial and illegal action'. Nevertheless, these dockers, their families, the Women of the Waterfront and their supporters picketed, campaigned and struggled for their re-instatement between September 1995 and January 1998. From the beginning of this dispute Dave Sinclair followed their struggle, capturing the good times and the bad times as this extraordinary section of the working class faded into a strange obscurity, largely ignored by the very movement they had led, the movement they had helped create in 1889.

In 1989 the Thatcher government abolished the National Dock Labour Scheme that covered some 9,400 registered dock workers. The number of registered dock workers employed in Liverpool and Birkenhead had fallen from 10,449 in 1970 to 1,244 in April 1989. By 1995, Liverpool docks employed just 420 former registered dock workers. The port of Liverpool, as with every other port in the country, was now back in the hands of port bosses who hired and fired casual, zero-hour workers as and when they were needed. The Liverpool docks dispute was the final struggle of former registered dockers against the iniquities of casual labour. The 1995 Liverpool dispute was the last stand of a section of the industrial working class that had fought since 1889 for better terms of conditions of employment and against casualisation. Len McCluskey, the UNITE General Secretary, and a former Liverpool dock worker, more recently compared casual labour with the contemporary scarcity of employment right and a living wage. He 'feared today's increasingly insecure economic climate, with growing numbers of people on short-term or zero-hours contracts', was a return to conditions he first witnessed as a young dock worker in Liverpool. 'It seems pretty clear to me that we are being taken back to what it was like on the docks, when men would gather first thing in the morning and the bosses would walk round and tap people on the shoulder and hand them a brass tally, meaning they had a day's work. When the bosses got bored they would throw the brass tallies in the air and I have seen men literally fight each other to get them because it meant the difference between putting food in their kids' bellies or them going hungry. We are heading back there again under this government with zero-hours contracts and it is no way to treat people or to give them a sense of dignity, a sense of belonging to a decent, respectful society.'

The Liverpool Dockers fought a heroic and revolutionary struggle that was as imaginative as it was radical. They had often struggled against their own union from its inception in 1889 to 1989 and they organised themselves valiantly as a rank and file organisation that was led by the Dockers, their 'de-recognised shop stewards, the Women of the Waterfront and an international movement of Dockers that took direct action in support of their Liverpool comrades. One of the sacked Liverpool Dockers, Andy Dwyer, was to reflect a year after the dispute had begun that, 'it is simply about an injustice, a total injustice about good men who gave a life to the dock industry to be just cast aside by somebody who is motivated by profit; it's about removing them scabs from my job. It is the biggest injustice in the Labour Movement since I can remember and people should be rallying behind, grasping this, rallying behind the Liverpool Dockers to make sure that they do win'. Ten years later Tony Benn MP was to state that 'The plain blunt truth is that the men and women of the waterfront fought a magnificent fight on the principle that you do not betray people who have been sacked by crossing a picket line …This dispute will be remembered in the history of the Labour Movement on the same scale and with the same honour as the Tolpuddle Martyrs and the Miners' Strike of 1984/85'. However, this heroic dispute, that began twenty years ago, has been largely forgotten and unrecorded by a movement and a Left that struggled to come to terms with the reality of the Liverpool Dockers struggle as it unfolded from September 1995. With one or two notable exceptions labour history has reduced this struggle of the Liverpool Dockers to vague footnotes or bland paragraphs of false solidarity.

Thankfully, the body of Dave Sinclair's work contradicts this trend, his photographs record a unique history, captured in real time, a history of portraits that shames others who have remained silent and who failed to respond when it was really needed in September 1995. Sinclair's often 'granite images' of these extraordinary men and women capture their power and physical strength as well as their dignity. Working always in black and white Dave Sinclair creates the sense these photographs have no timeframe, they could have been the same Liverpool Dockers' images recorded in another century. One of his most iconic images is of Jack Heyman, one of the rank and file leaders of the International Longshoremen, (ILWU), flanked, either side, by the two leaders of the Liverpool Dockers, Jimmy Nolan and Jimmy Davies. It is a wonderful image of three comrades crossing continents in every way possible. This simple photograph locks in a wonderful moment of hard men, good comrades sharing a moment of real solidarity and joy.

Above all, as the sole chronicler of the Liverpool Dockers at this time Dave Sinclair was a friend of the Dockers and their families and he became the 'official photographer' of the Liverpool dock dispute – but more than this Dave Sinclair was seen as a comrade trusted by all the Dockers and their families to 'record the truth'. Some of the wonderful images in this book are the narrative of this historic dispute. A class that was physically related and connected to the same Dockers who began their history of struggle in 1889. This book is a tribute to the men and women who fought this radical fight. Many of the Dockers and their families, who took part in this struggle lost everything they had. This book captures the iron and the soul of these brave men and women and their supporters, providing us all with a record and an insight into the dignity of a class that will never exist again in the form it once held.

ACKNOWLEDGEMENTS

My thanks go to Ken Loach for his foreword and to Mike Carden, Jimmy Nolan, Doreen McNally and Sally Stein on behalf of Allan Secula for their contributions. Mike Carden will be publishing a complete history of the Dockers' dispute in the near future.

Tony Nelson, Kevin Robinson and the Shop Stewards' Committee for their invaluable help. Jimmy Davies Junior for his contribution to my Flikr site.

The activists and curators who have not allowed this body of work to be forgotten. Thanks to Emma Ferguson, Elizabeth Watts and Jenny Stephens for helping me make this book happen.

Most of all my thanks go to the Dockers on the picket lines who welcomed me, a wonderful group of men who I am proud to have photographed.

I regret there were some very important people who do not appear in the book, and I apologise for any wrong names.

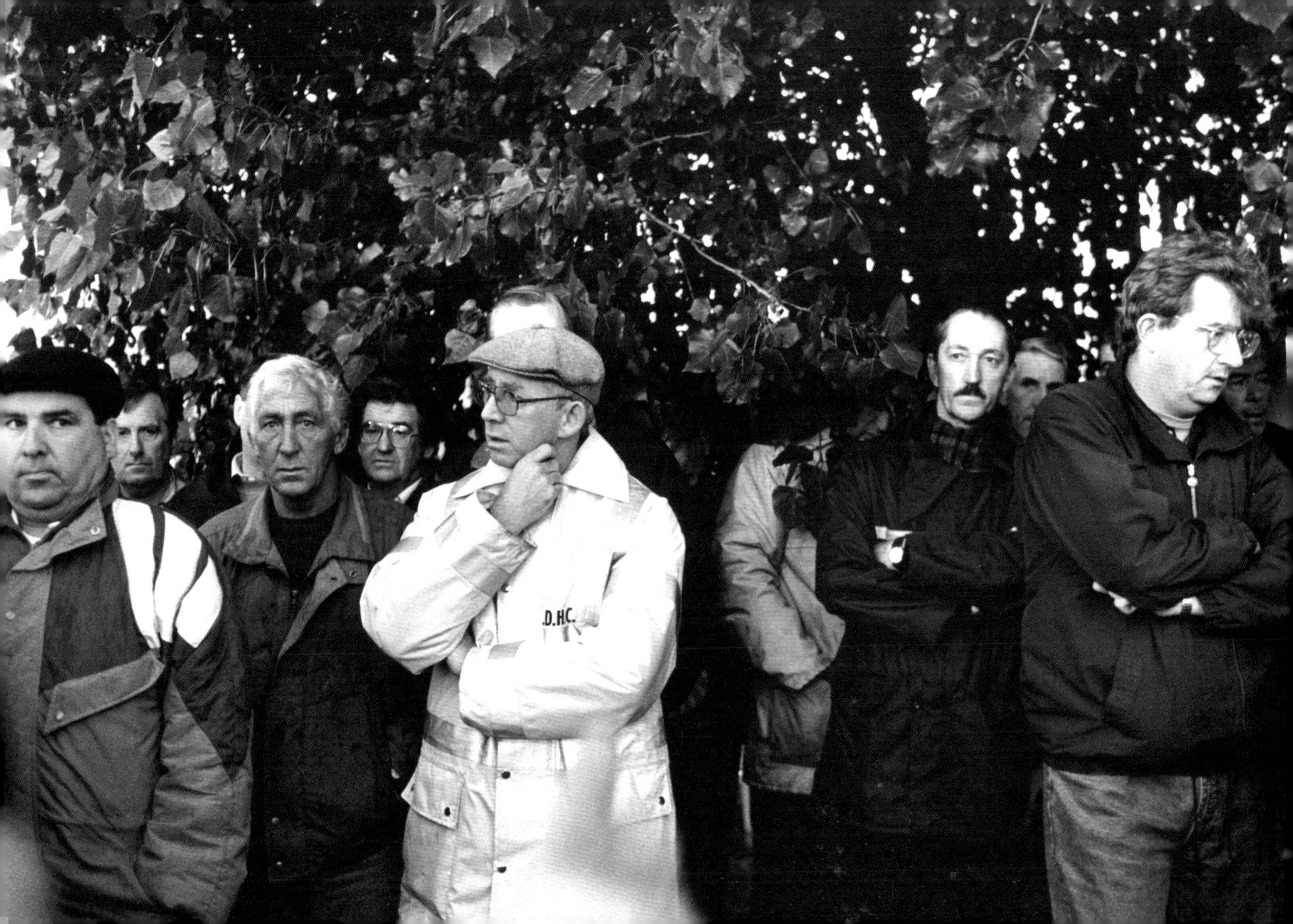
.D.H.C.

Above: Early morning at the Gladstone Gate.

Right: March to the Seaforth Gate.

Opposite: First morning of the Seaforth picket, 28 September 1995.

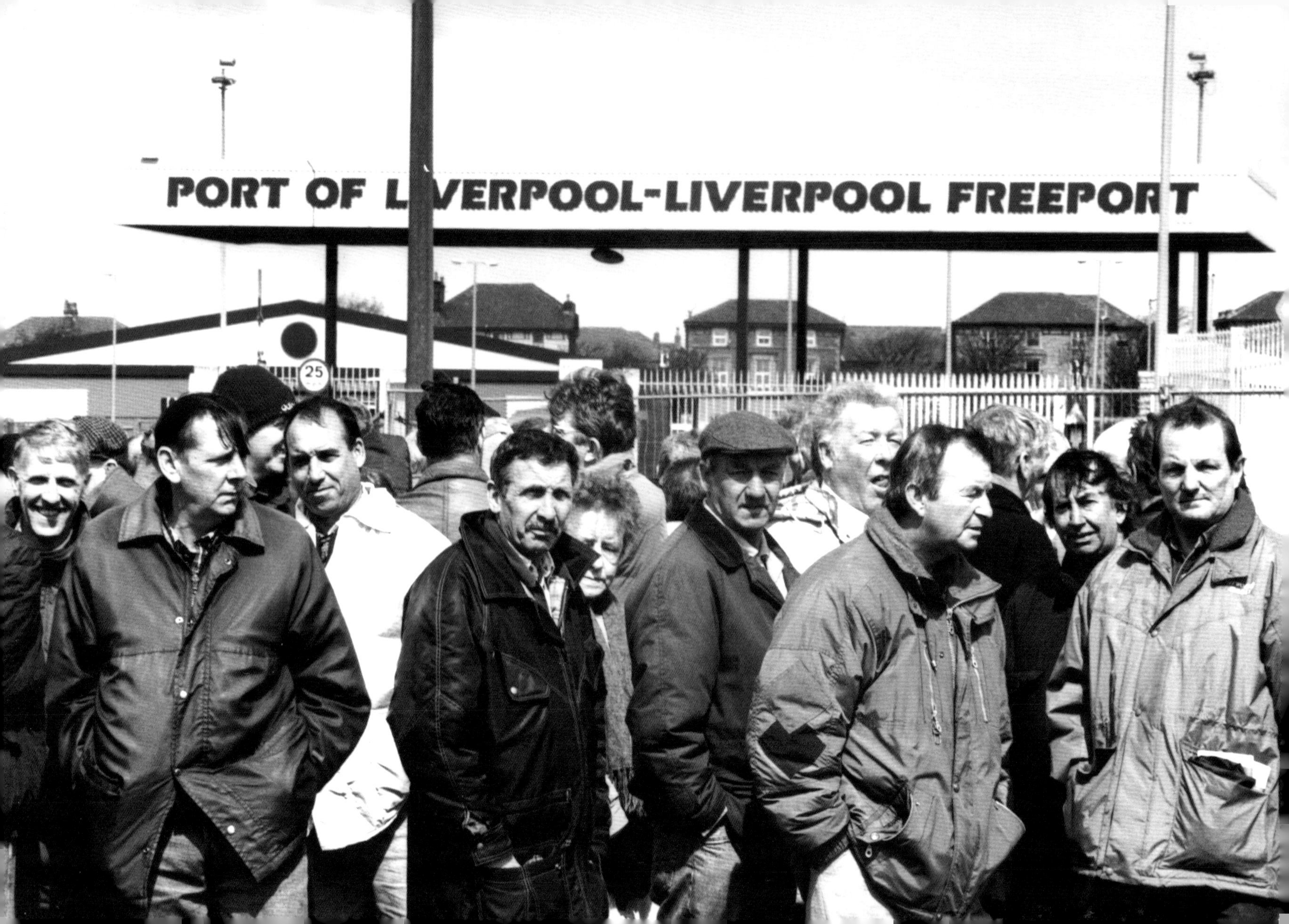
PORT OF LIVERPOOL-LIVERPOOL FREEPORT
25

Above: Billy Bragg.

Above right: Ronnie, Charlie and Nick, Seaforth, late '95.

Below right: Mark at the Norse Irish Gate.

Opposite: Blocking the Seaforth Gate.

Scabby Mally walks through a picket line at Seaforth Container Terminal.

Torside men at an early mass meeting, October '95.

Dockers' families attend a demo in '95.

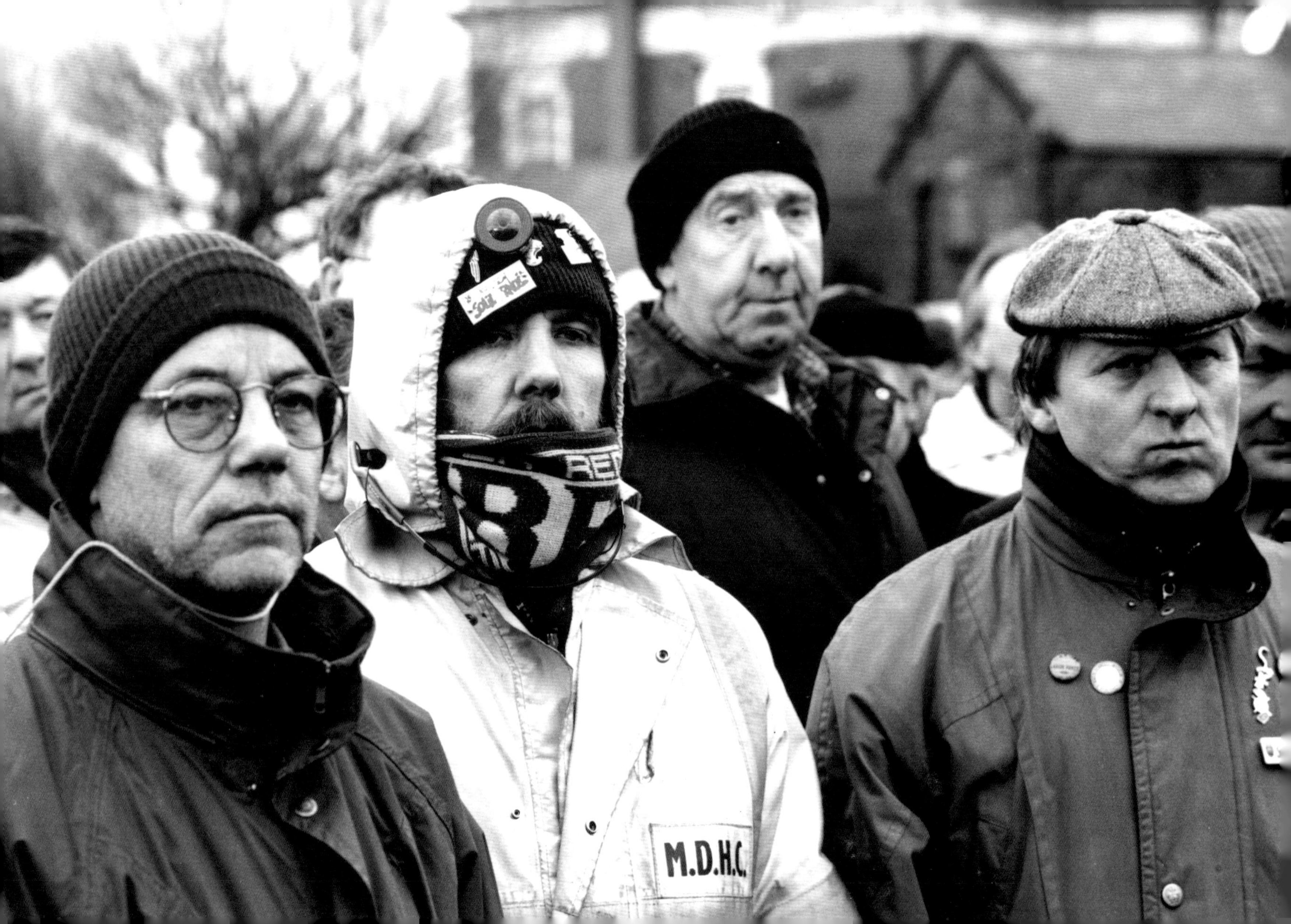
M.D.H.C.

Above: Marty Size.

Above right: Tony Nelson on a Seaforth picket.

Below right: Jimmy Dempsey watches scabs.

Opposite: Davey, Mick, Tommy and Mick. Seaforth, '95.

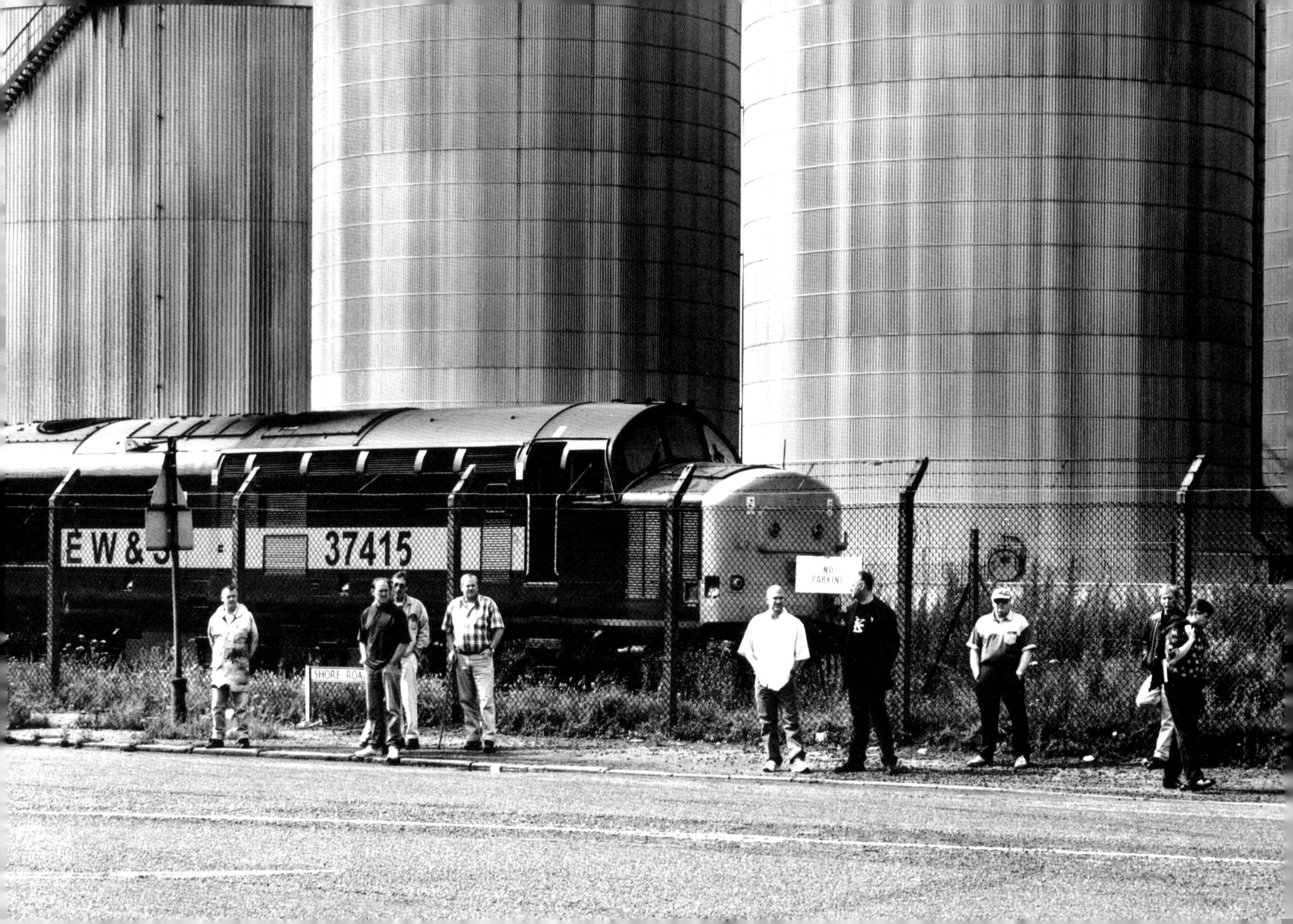
EW&S
37415
NO PARKING
SHORE ROA

Above: Joe, Mike, Kevin, Stevie, Tony and Jimmy. Seaforth, '95.

Right: Dockers' children on demonstration of support, Liverpool, '95.

Opposite: Dockers on the Dock Road.

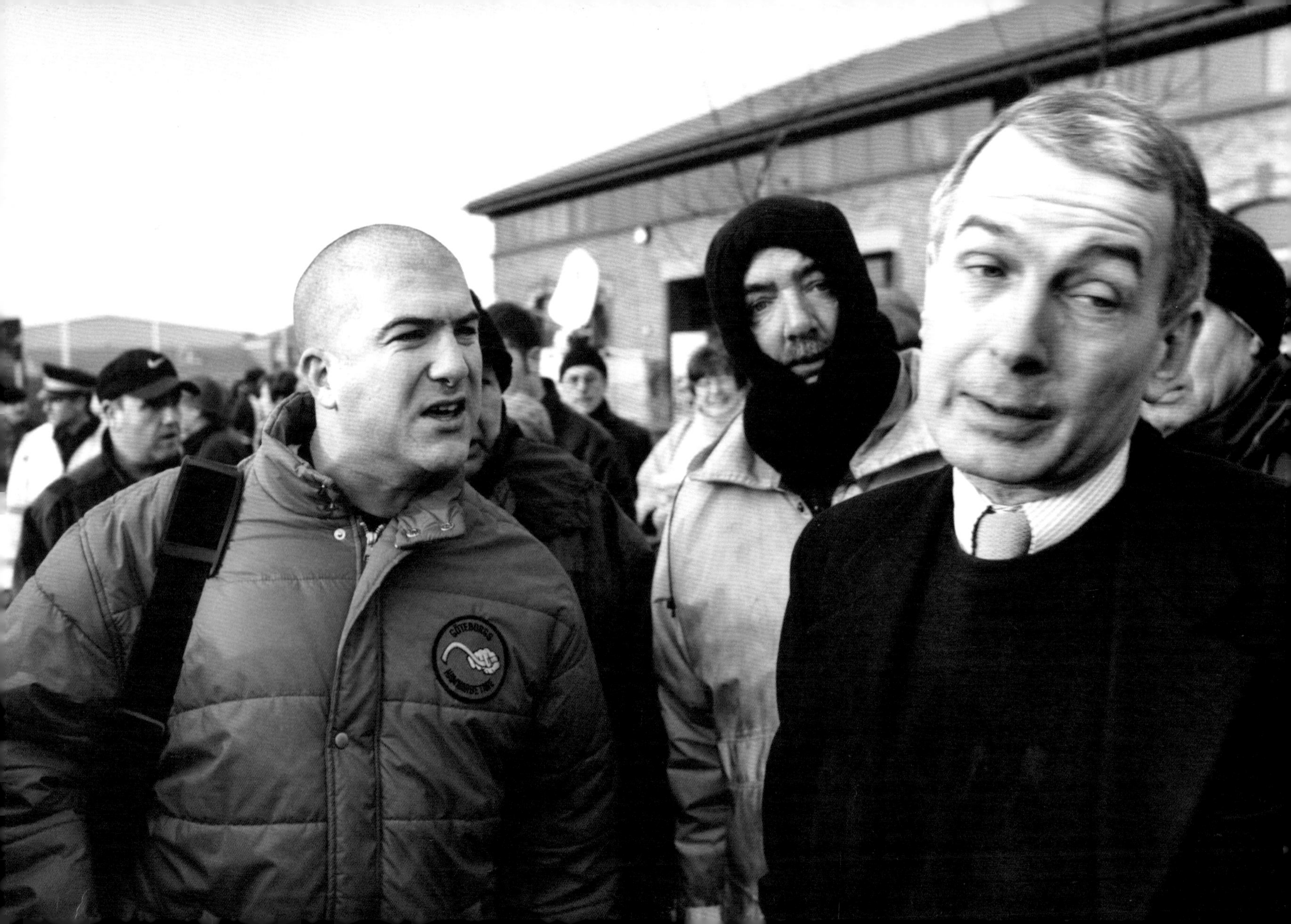
GÖTEBORGS

Above: Tony Benn and Jimmy Nolan speaking at an early demo in support of the dockers, '95.

Opposite: Jimmy Davies Jnr has a go at his MP Frank Field for his lack of support, Birkenhead, '98.

Joe McMahon was sacked while he was on holiday.

Above: Alan Loy and Larry Riley.

Opposite: Dockers walk home after early morning picket.

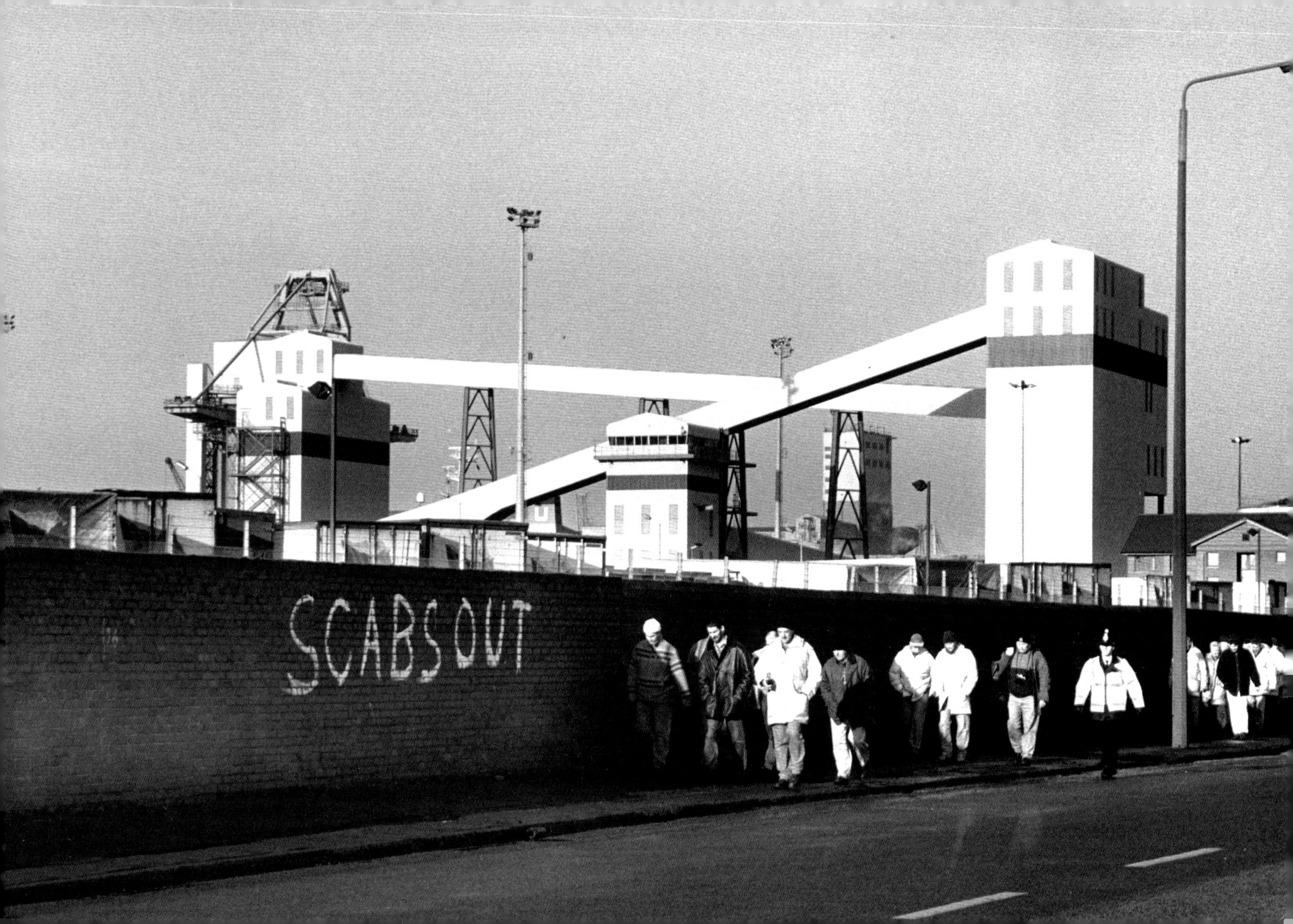
SCABS OUT

Above: Ken Loach during the making of his documentary *The Flickering Flame*.

Opposite: The first mass picket of the Seaforth Gate, '95.

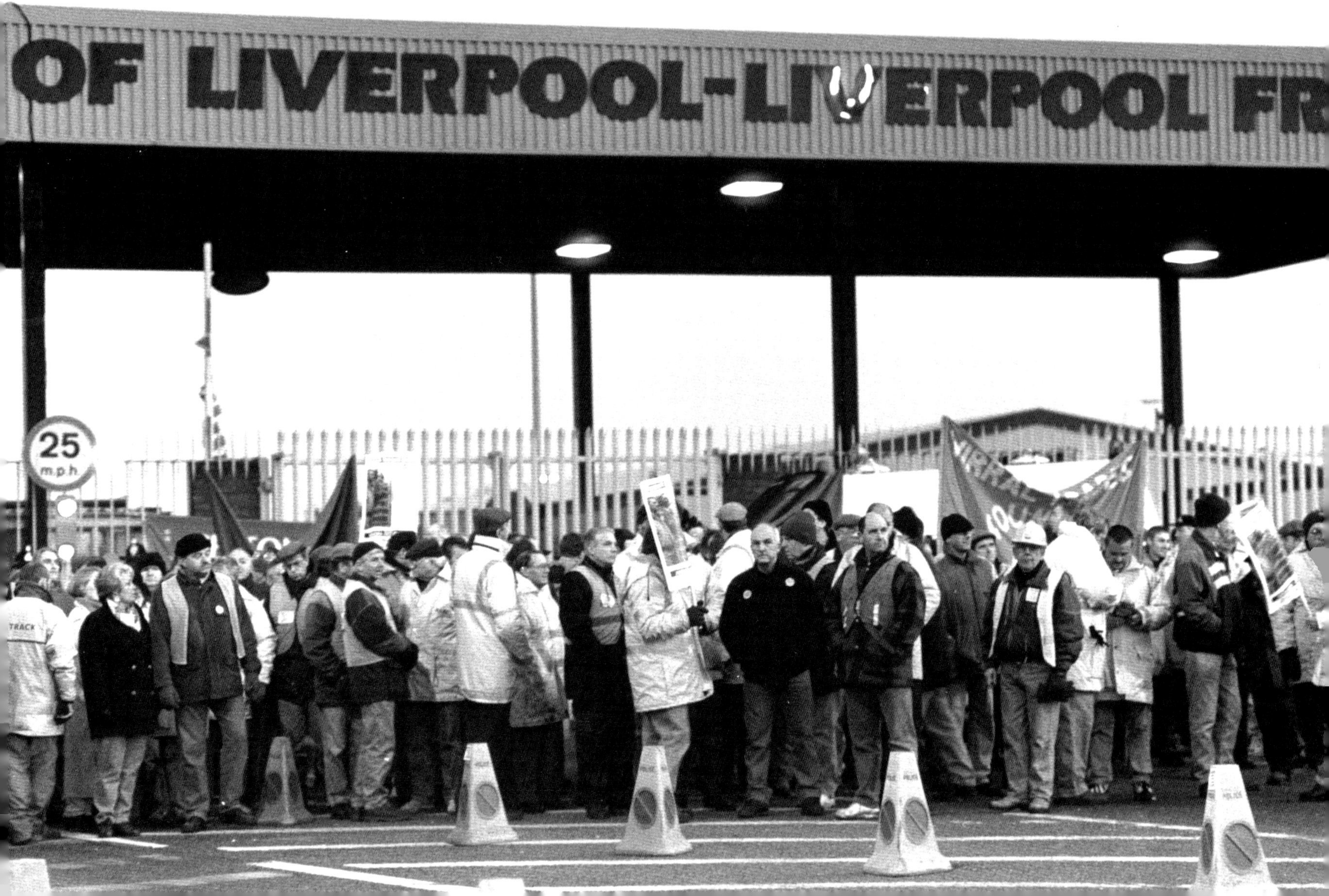
OF LIVERPOOL-LIVERPOOL
25
m.p.h.

Left: Torside men and Kevin Robinson at the first morning picket at Seaforth.

Opposite: Blocking the Norse Irish Gate, '95.

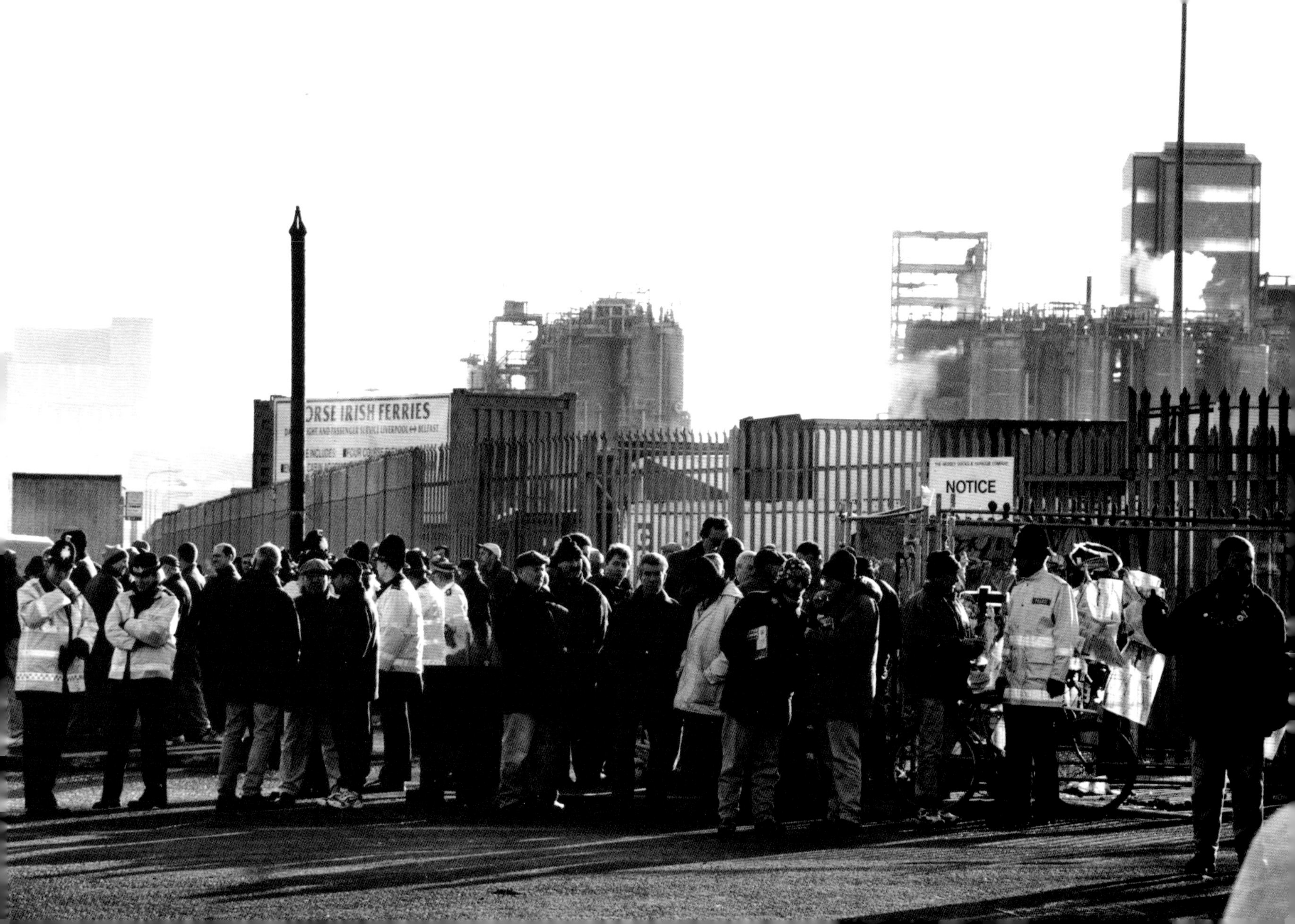
ORSE IRISH FERRIES
NOTICE

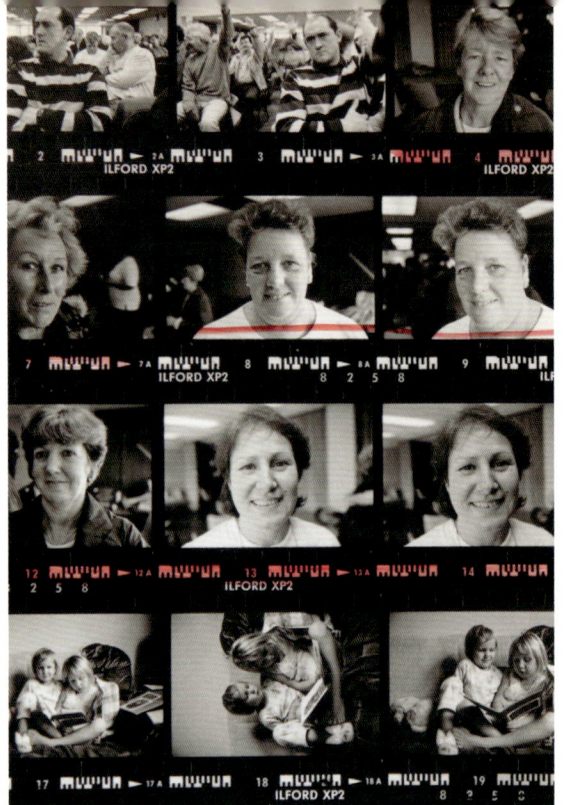

Above: Women of the Waterfront.

Above left: Doreen McNally among the Women of the Waterfront on a wet, early morning picket.

Below left: Women in Dispute from Hillingdon Hospital in London come to Liverpool to offer support.

Opposite left: Dockers stop a train on the Dock Road.

Opposite right: Scab Port.

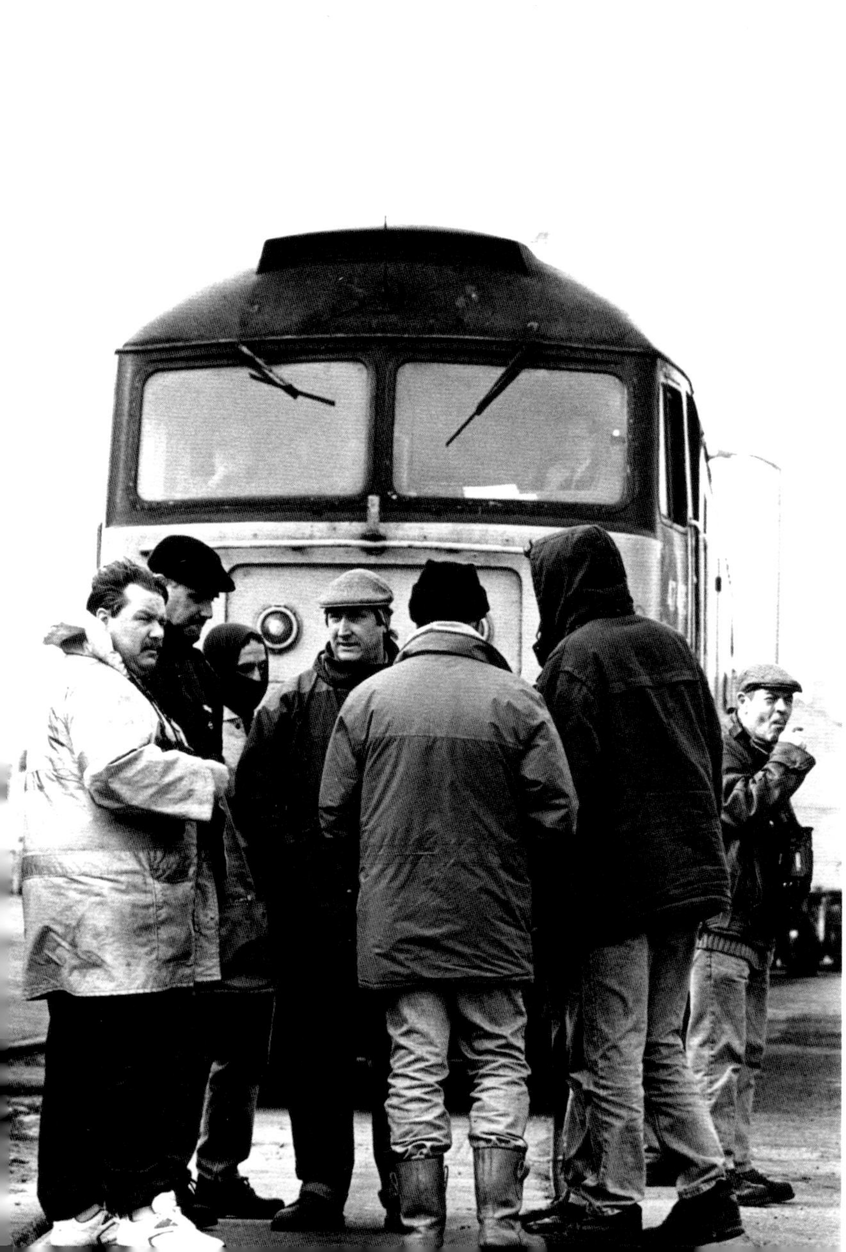

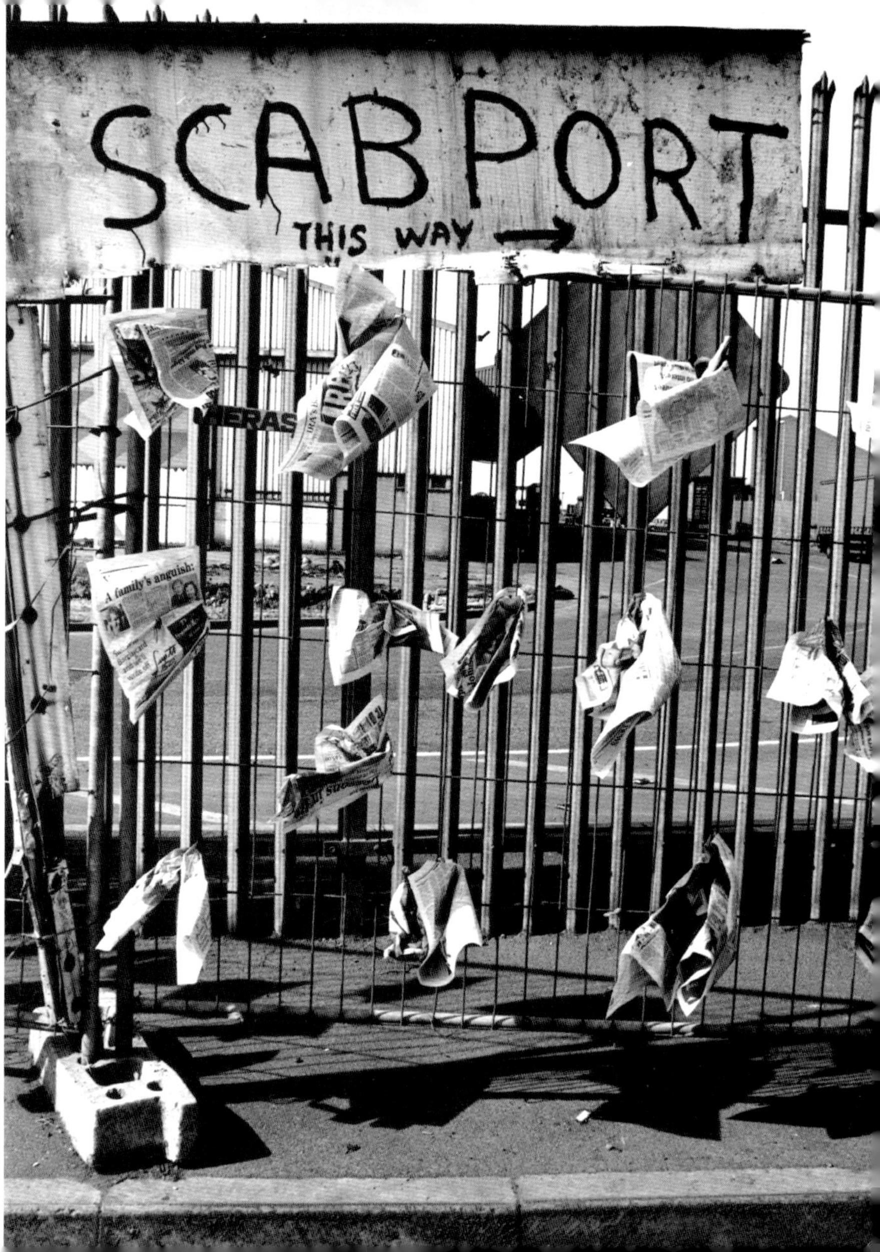
SCABPORT
THIS WAY
A family's anguish:

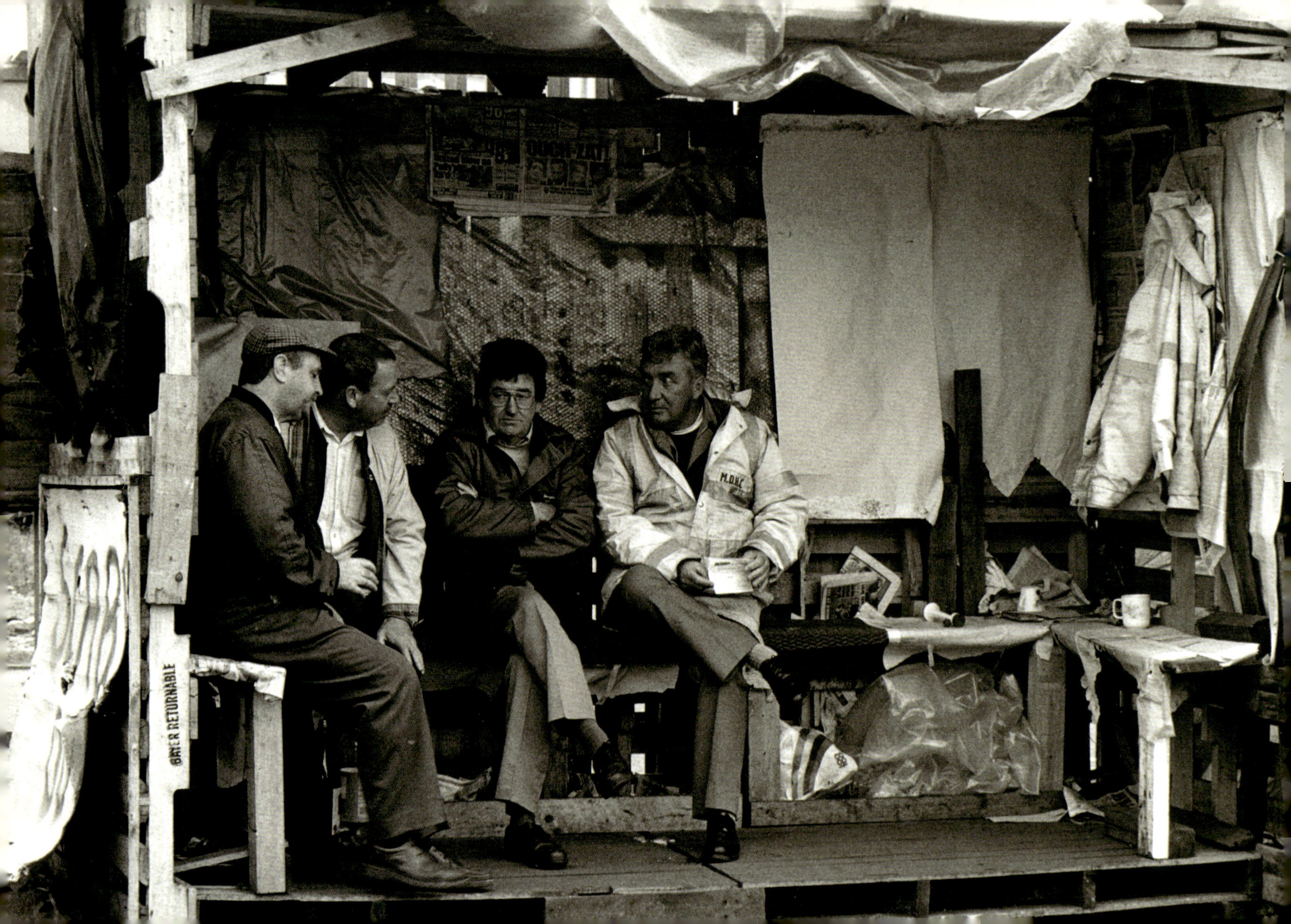
OUCH-ZAT!
M.D.H.C
RETURNABLE

Above: Jimmy Campbell.

Below right: John, Mark, Tony, John and Tony at a mass meeting, '95.

Opposite: George, Tommy, Cliff and Wally.

MERSEYSIDE DOCK LABOURERS
T & G
SHOP STEWARDS' COMMITTEE
ROLLS-ROYCE
Bristol
TEST AREAS
LANCASHIRE
WOMEN AGAINST
SEFTON
KNOWSLEY
UNISON
T G W U
CREWE BRANCH
6/759
6/523
P-E
KIRKBY

Above: Danny, Jimmy and Eddie Loyden, MP for Garston.

Above right: First banner made by the newly formed Women of the Waterfront, Dockers' wives, daughters and mothers based on the Miners' Wives movement from the '84/85 Miners' Strike.

Below right: Women of the Waterfront.

Opposite: Mayday at the Town Hall, '96.

Les, Frank, Steve and Eddy.

Kevin Flynn watching scabs.

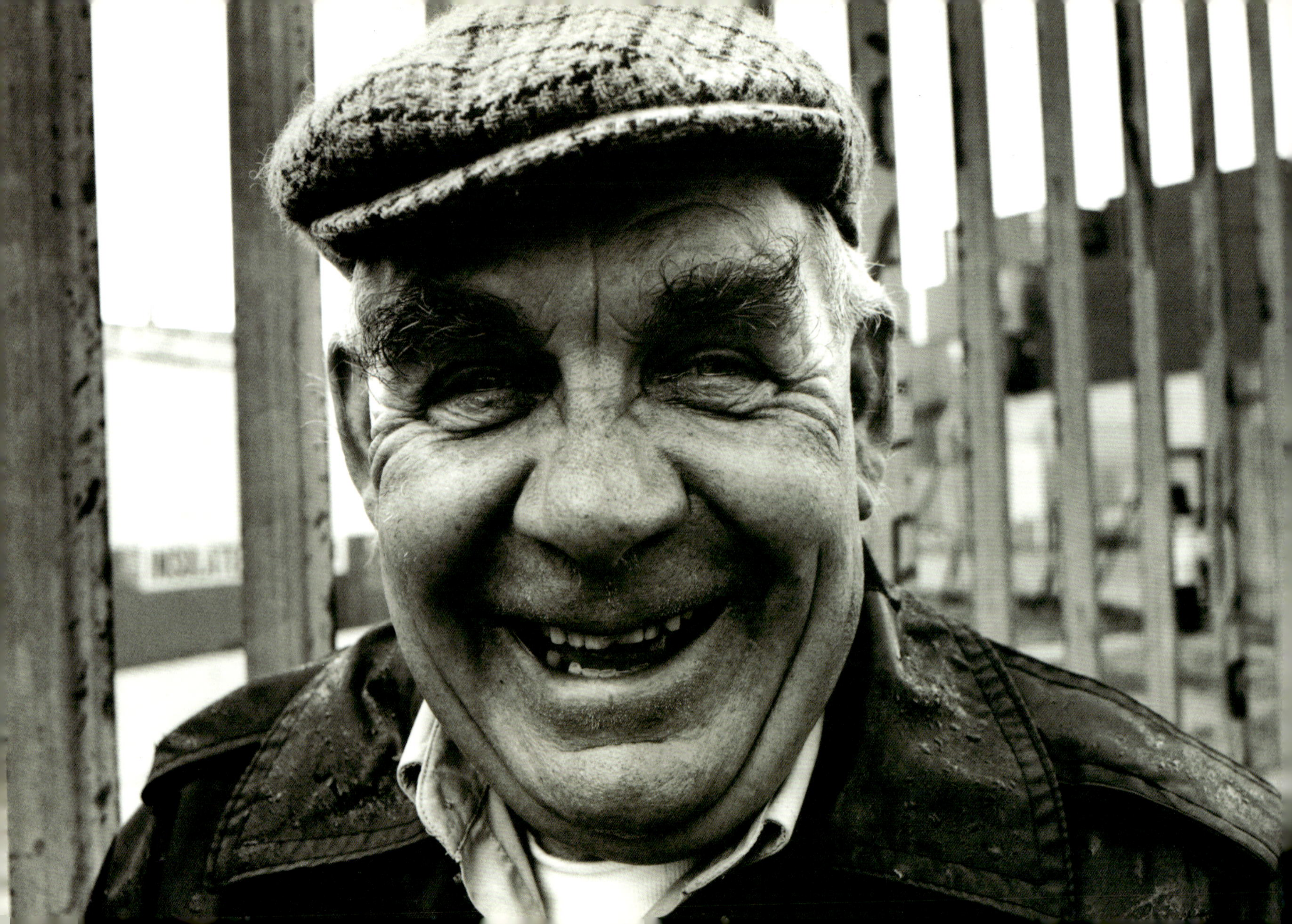

Above: Jimmy Davies Junior among Torside lads at one of the Friday mass meetings.

Above right: Bob Ritchie, Mike Carden, Frank Lanigan, Bill Morris, Jimmy Nolan, John Bowers, Tommy Gleeson and Bobby Morton. Bill Morris was speaking about how the T&G would support the Dockers but they never did. (Bowers and Gleeson were from the USA East Coast docks union, the ILA.)

Below right: Corbyn Pilger.

Opposite: Brownie, a retired docker and former member of the 'Blue Union' giving support on the picket line.

Jacko, Joe, Stevie, Nat and Terry on the Norse Irish Gate picket.

Norse Irish Gate.

Seaforth Gate.

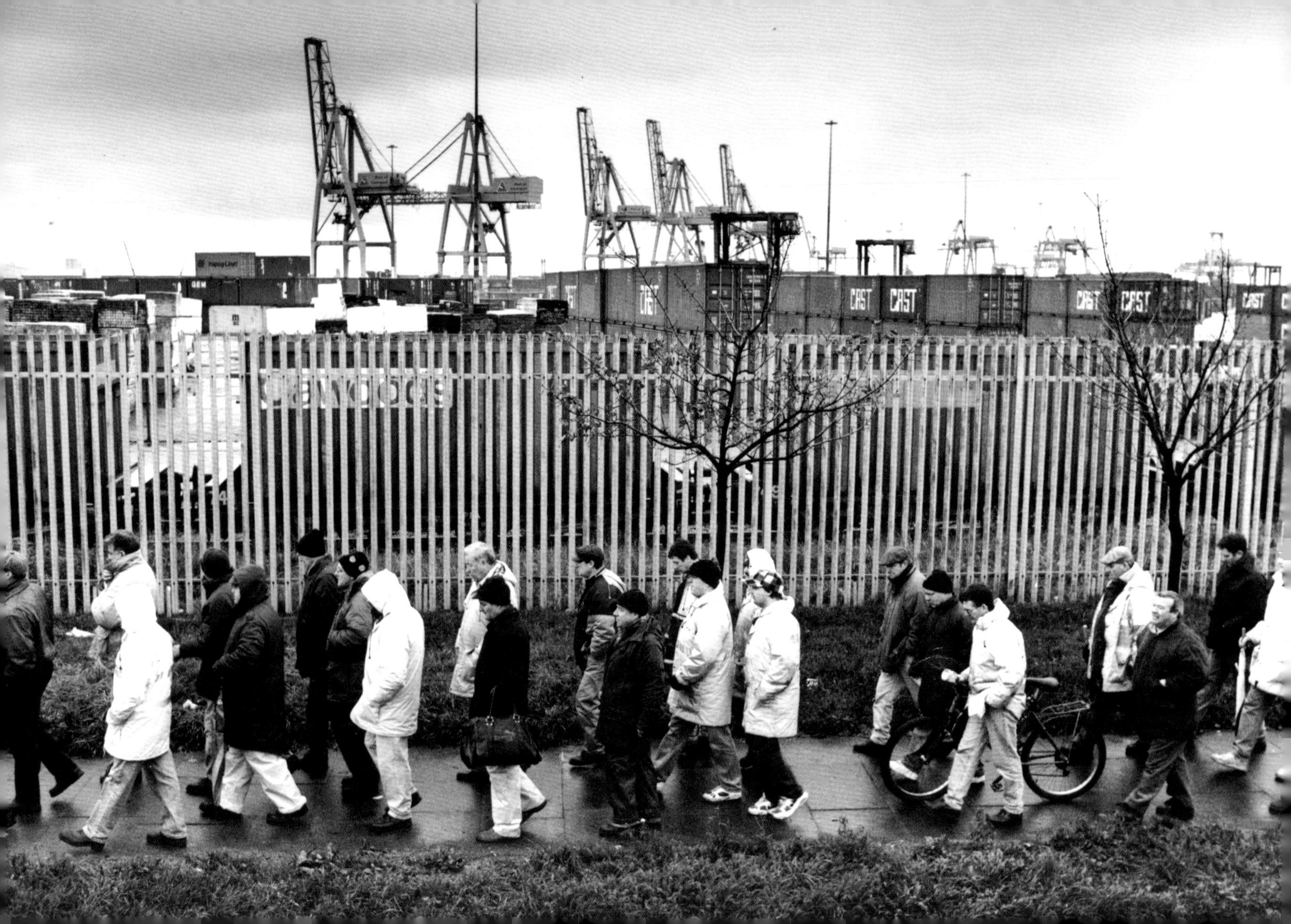
CAST

Above: Scab hides his face from Joe.

Above right: Occupation of Norse Irish Terminal to confront scabs.

Below right: Irvine Welsh.

Opposite: Walking home after early morning Seaforth picket.

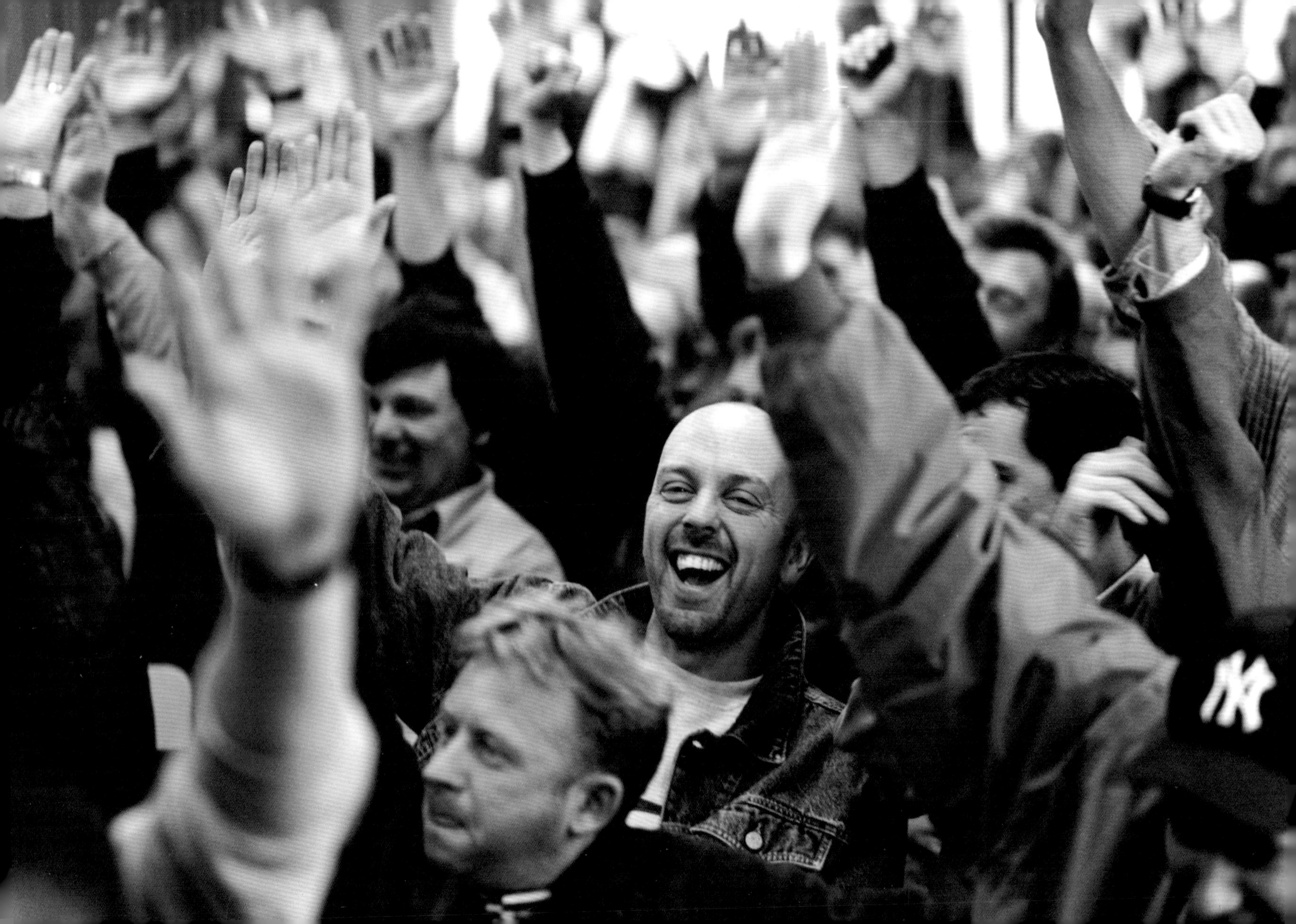
NY

Above: International visitors.

Above right: Tony Atkins and John Ryan at the front of a demo through London, Christmas '96.

Below right: Demonstration of international supporters marches to Seaforth from Liverpool.

Opposite: Tony Melia voting to stay in dispute at a weekly mass meeting.

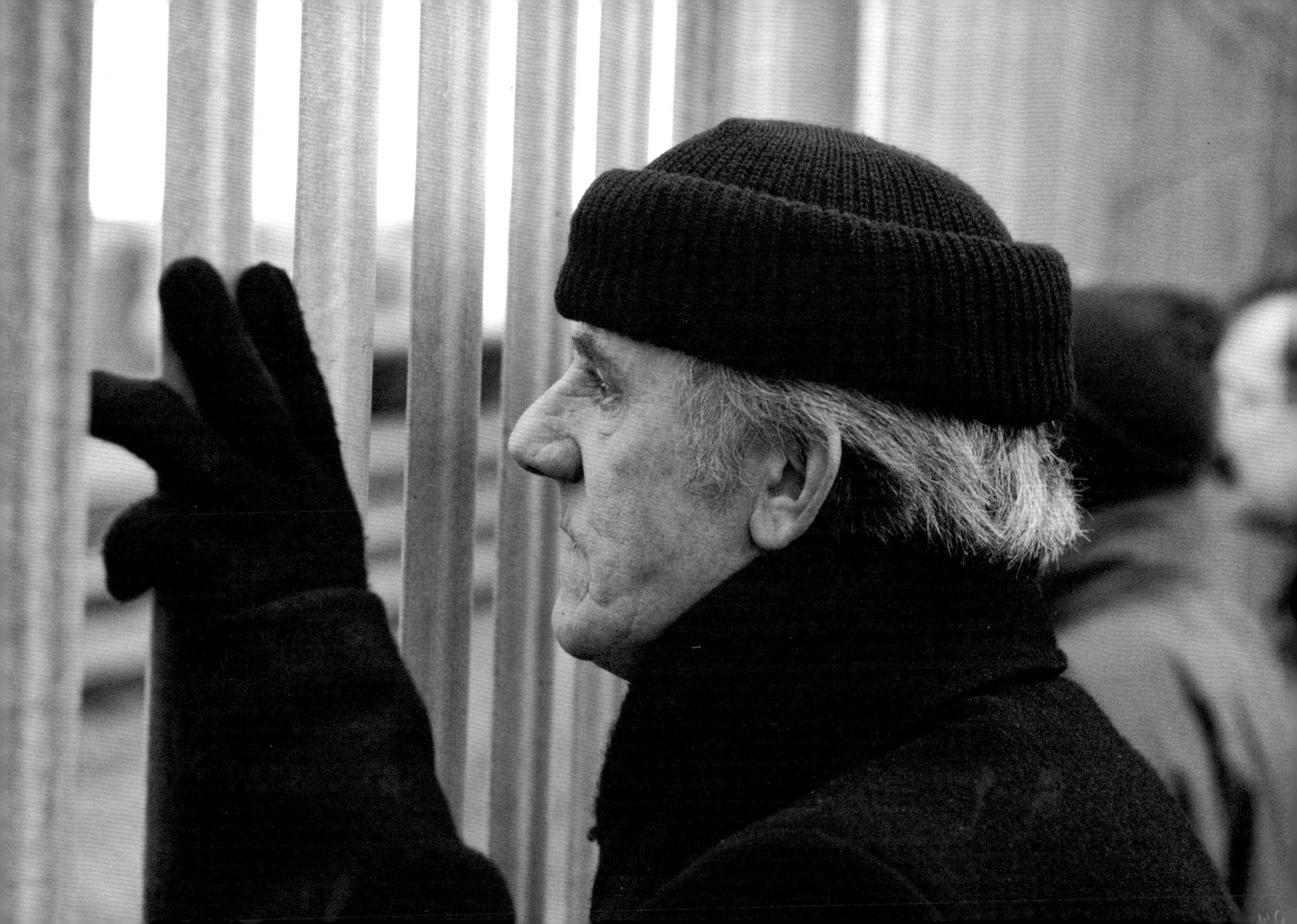

Above: Andy Dwyer watching scabs.

Right: A Dockers' daughter and granddaughter at a rally of support.

Opposite: Billy Williams watching scabs do his job.

Tommy.

Gerry Smythe.

Women of the Waterfront at a mass meeting during speeches by international visitors.

ME AND MY DAD HATE SCABS

Tommy and George.

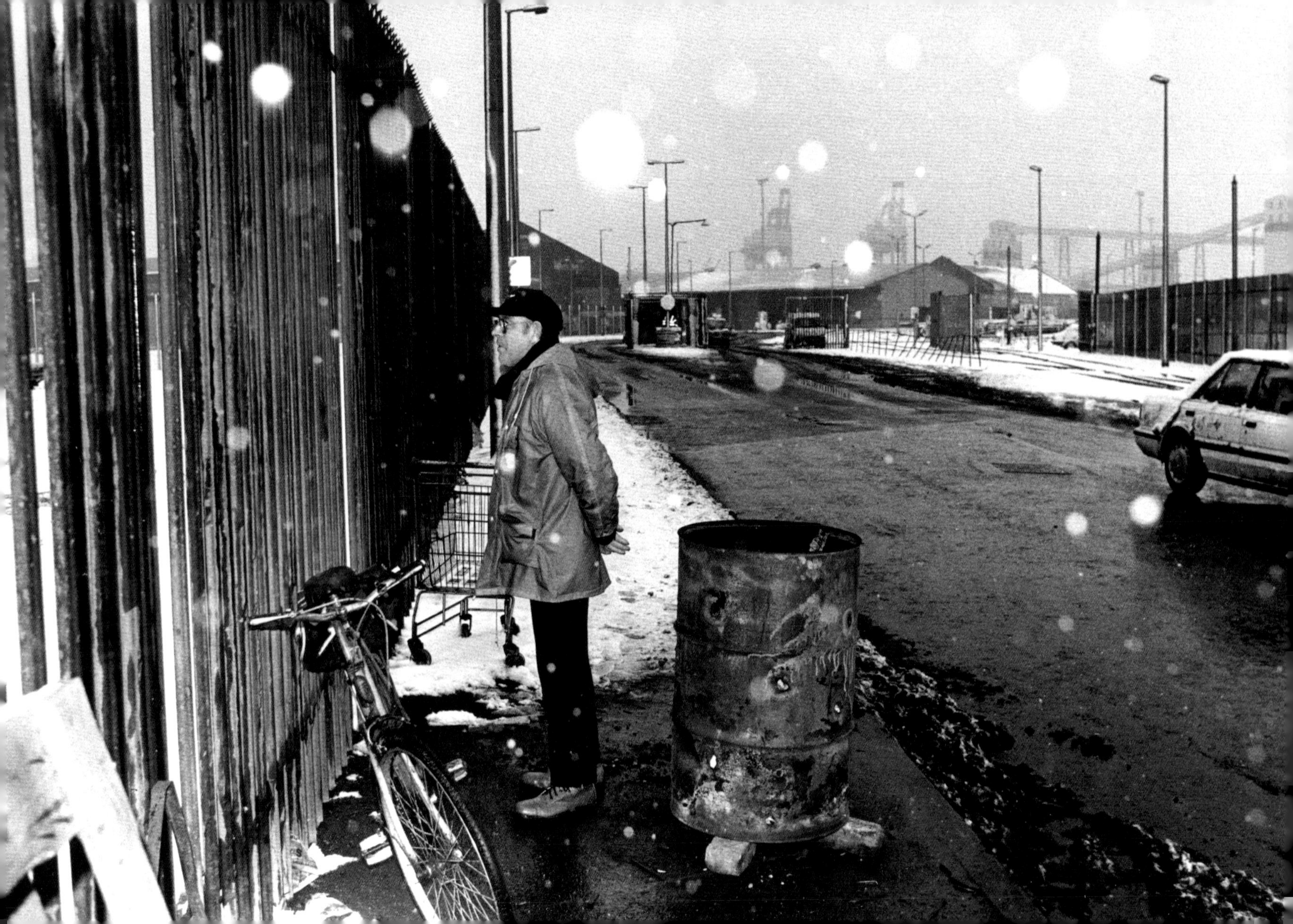

Jimmy Davies, Jack Heyman (USA West Coast Dockers' union leader, ILWU) and Jimmy Nolan.

Above: Dockers' kids listen to speeches at Dock Road rally.

Opposite: Gordon O'Keefe.

Larry shows an International delegate his father's maritime logbooks at the Dockers' Club.

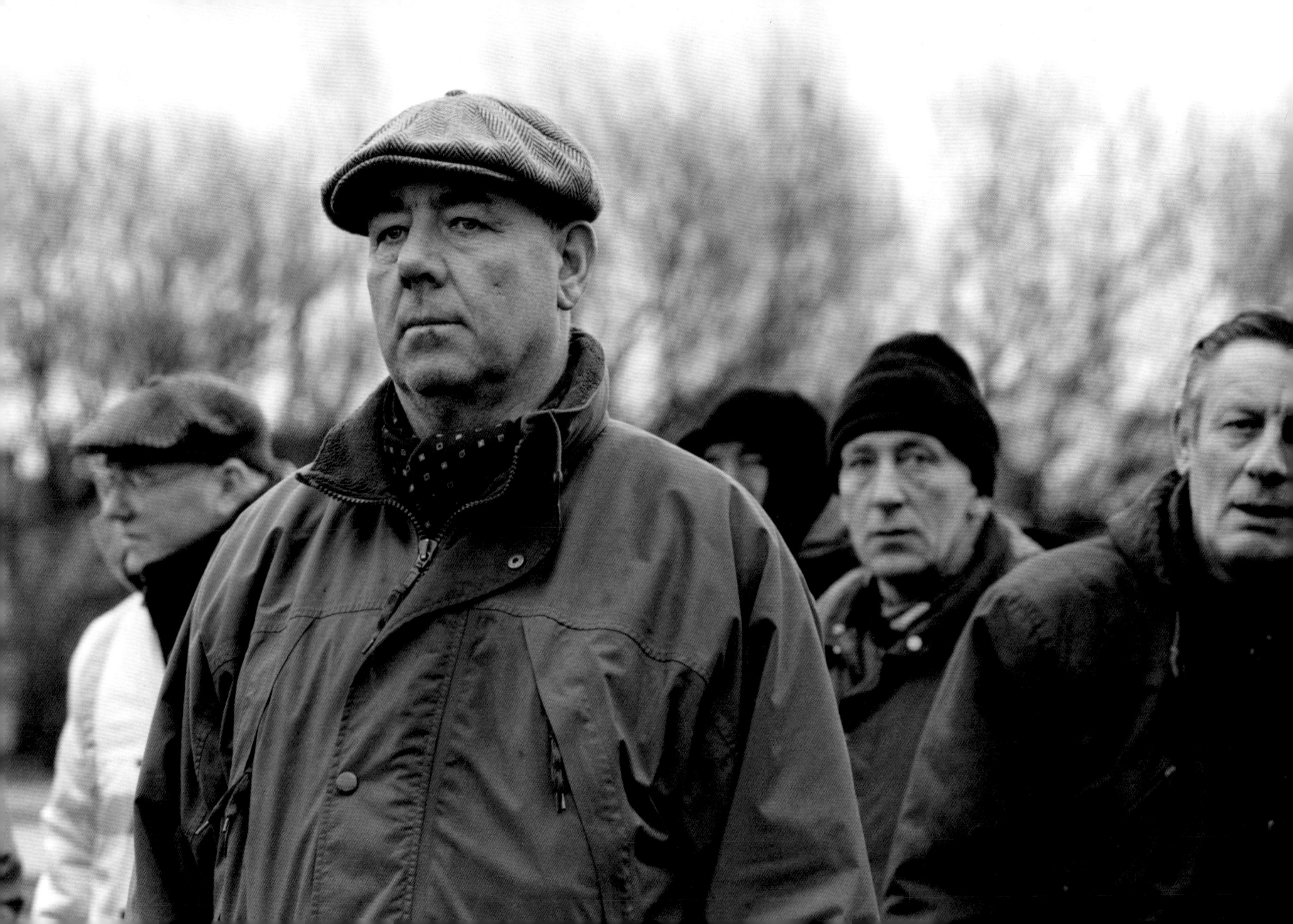

Above: Sammy, John, Neil, John and Larry let a scab know what they think.

Right: Tony Boothe.

Opposite: Dennis Connolly.

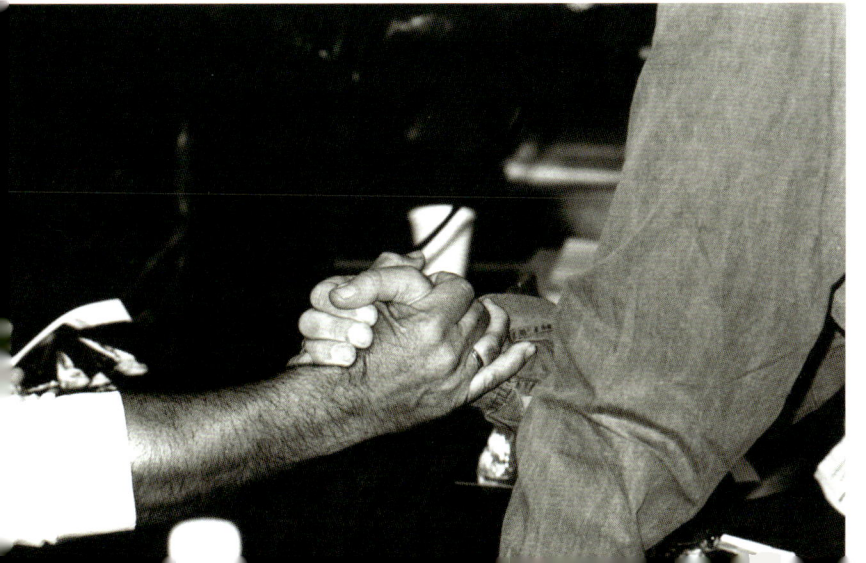

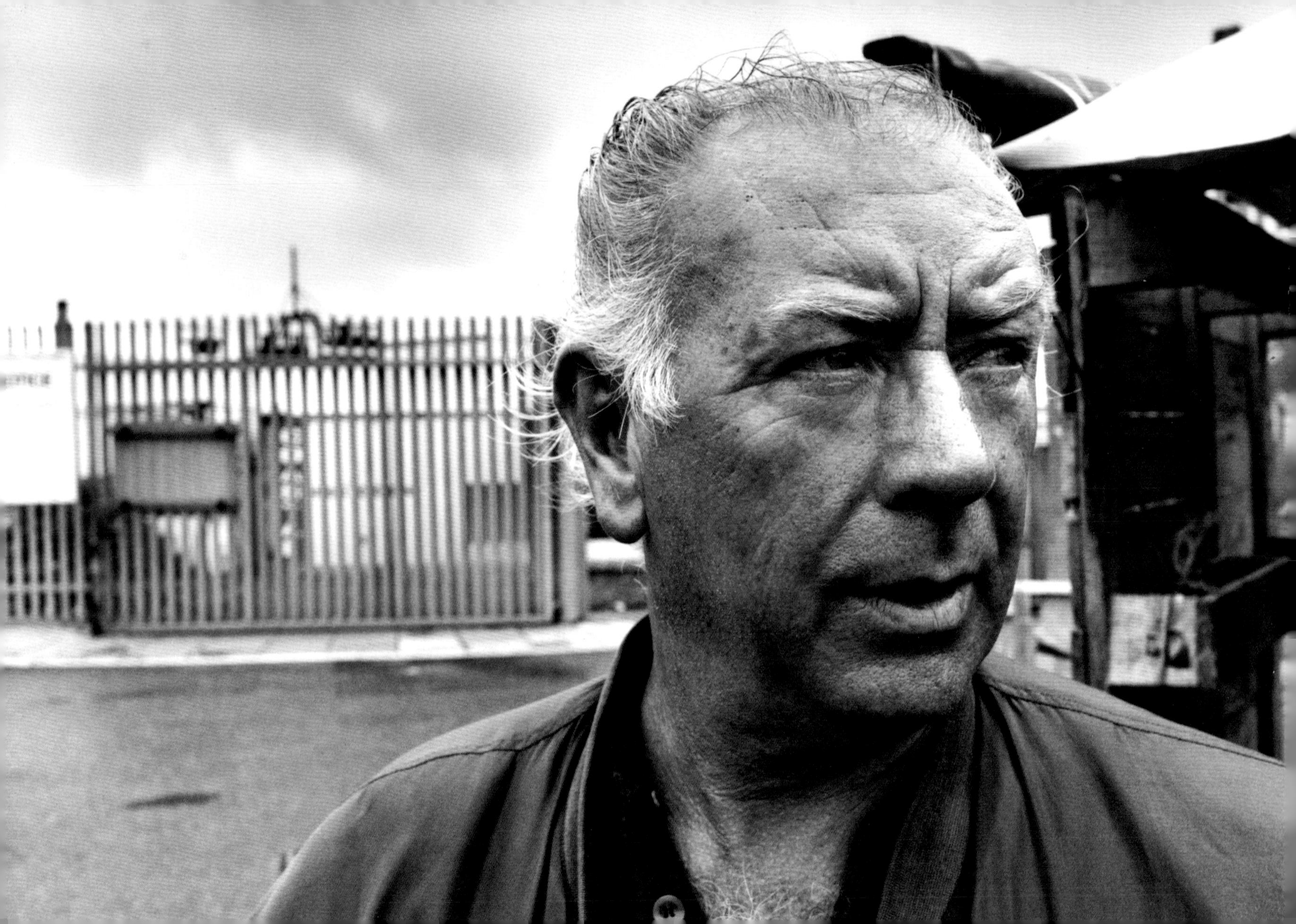

Above: Ina at the T&G saying goodbye before going back to Australia.

Above right: Ina from Australia joins the WOW at Seaforth Gate picket.

Below right: Author.

Opposite: Nat Givvons.

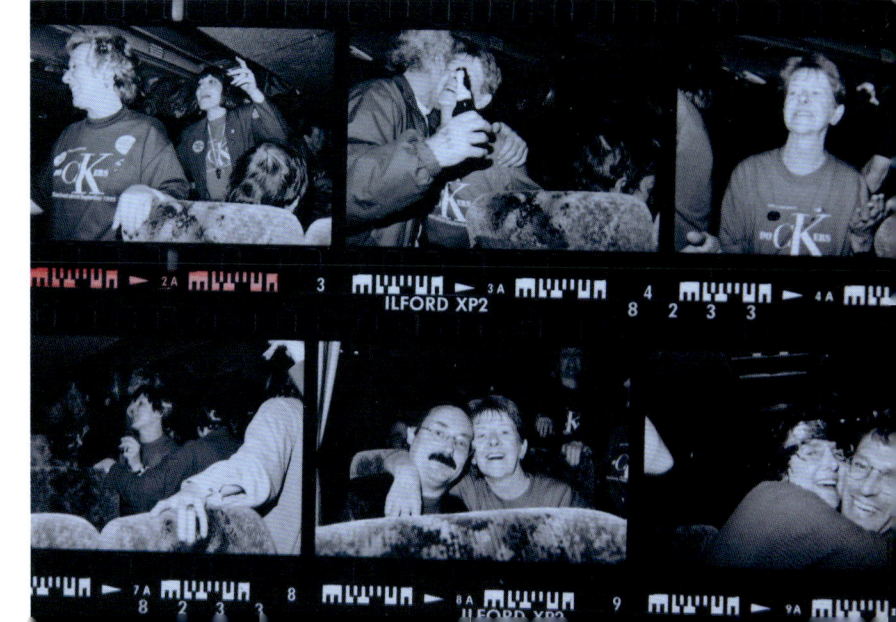

Stopping a truck at the Gladstone Dock Gate.

Opposite: Winter '97.

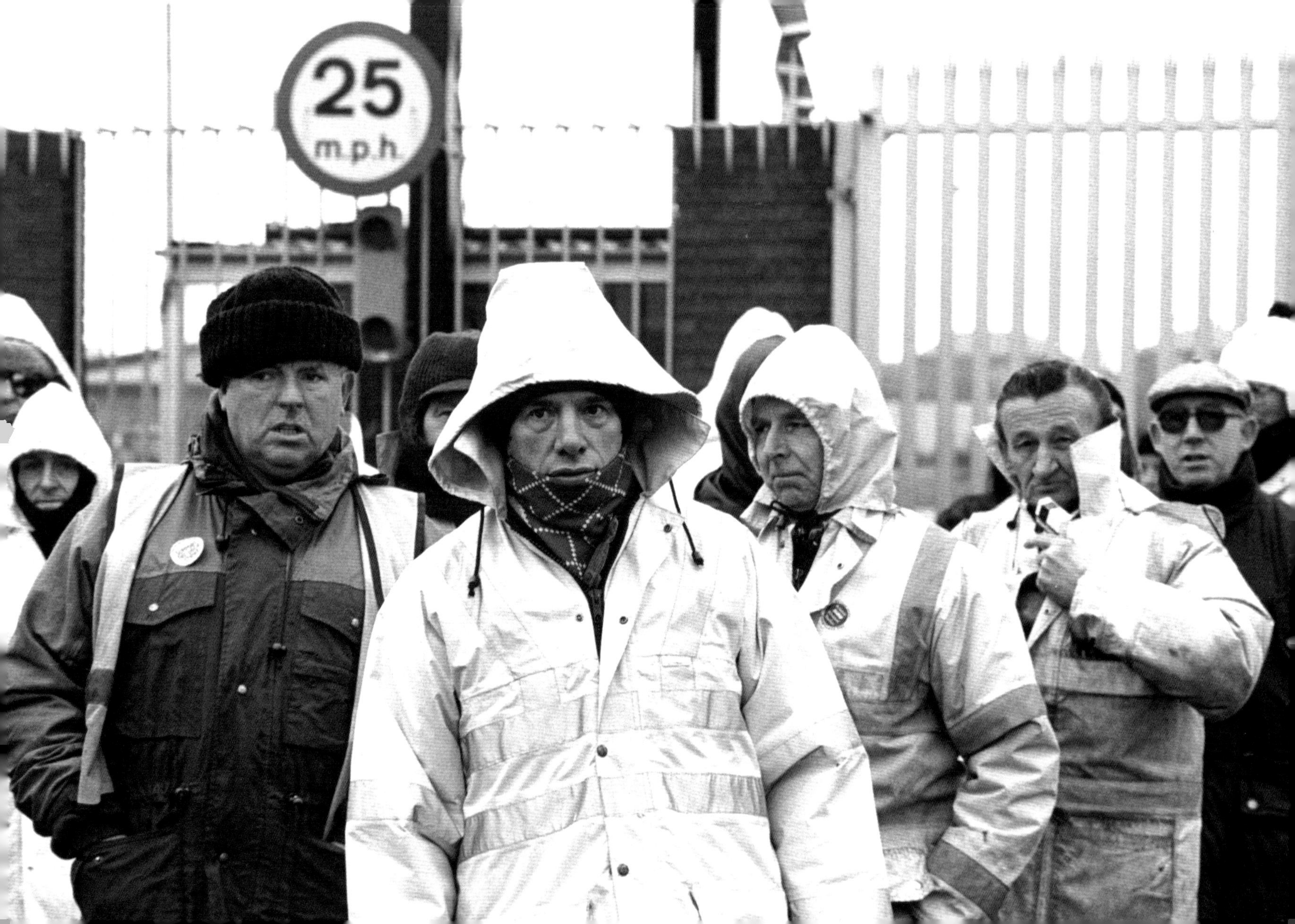
25
m.p.h.

Left: Paco and Rico at a rally of international delegates supporting the Liverpool Dockers. Paco later died in a ship accident in Tenerife.

Opposite: Peter Stroud.

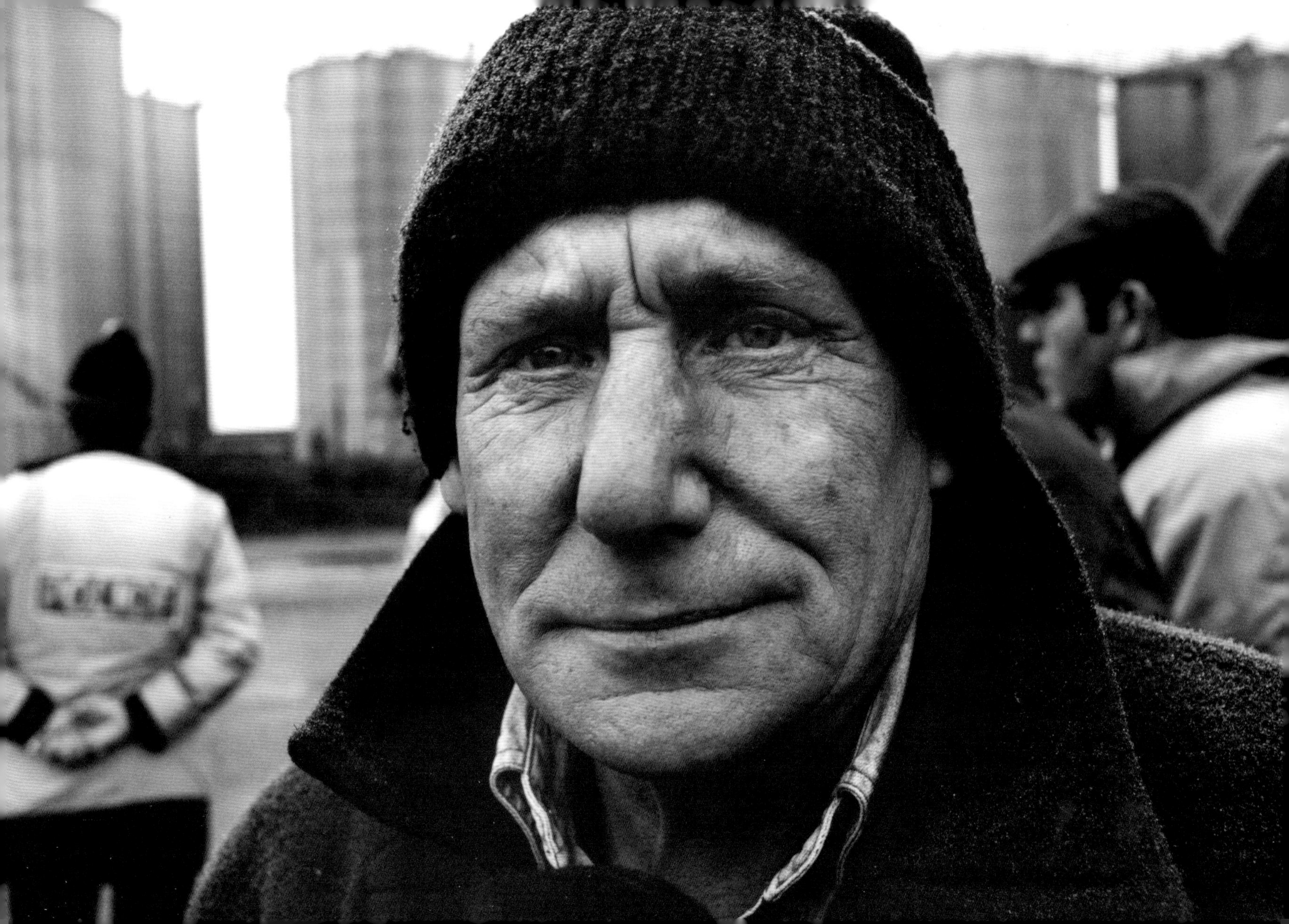

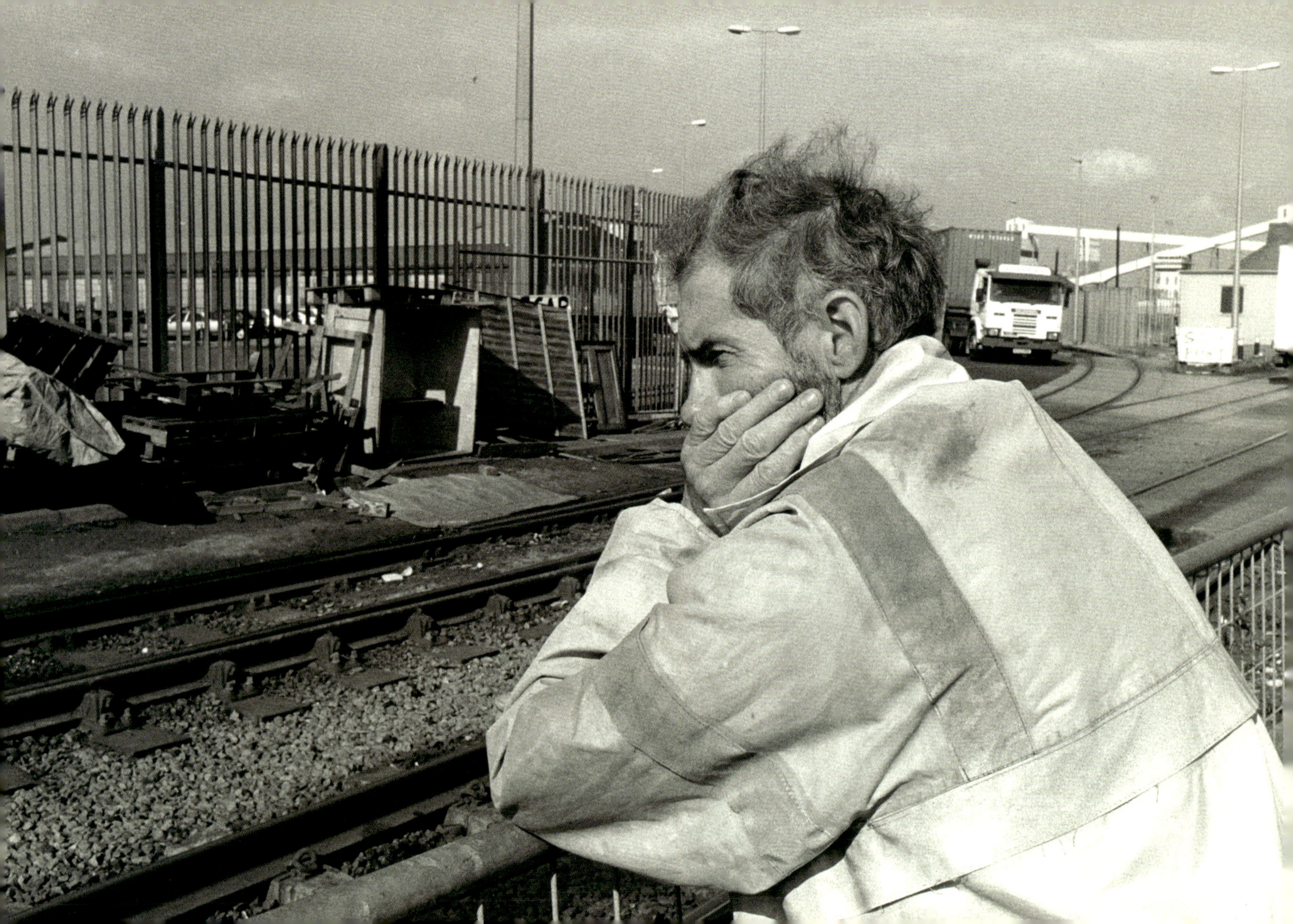

Right: Seaforth.

Opposite: Jacky Guy.

Billy Dunne carried by workmates from the Norse Irish Ferries.

Mick Kilcullen.

Gordon O'Keefe and Georgie Preston.

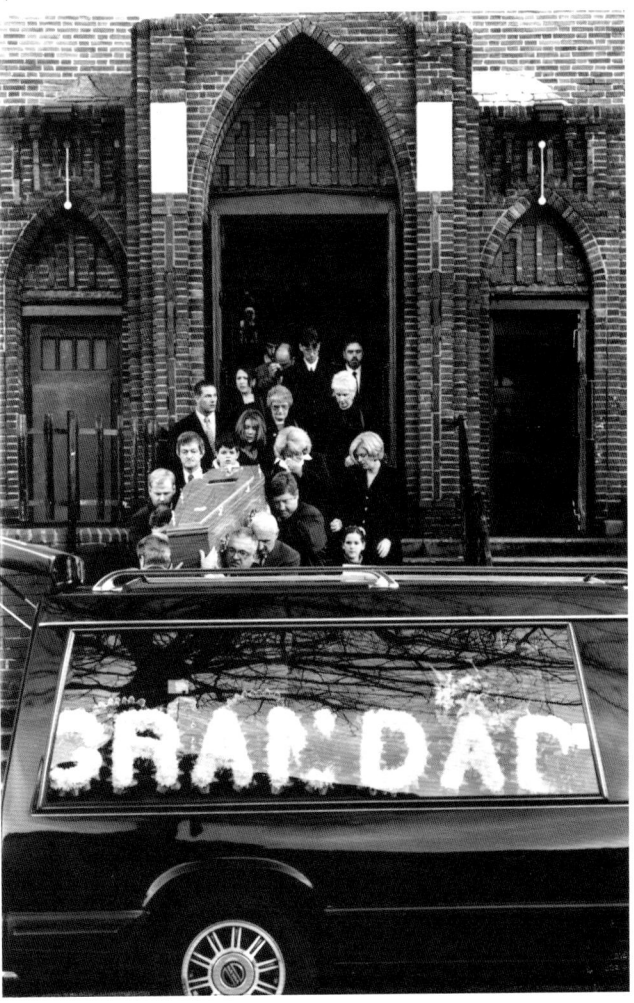

Billy Roonie and his funeral.

ASSOCIATED SOCIETY of LOCOMOTIVE ENGINEERS & FIREMEN
1880
PROGRESS
ASSOCIATED SOCIETY OF
LOCOMOTIVE ENGINEERS & FIREMEN
LEEDS 116 BRANCH
BRENT

Dockers support postal workers when postal managers drive vans through picket lines at Copras Hill sorting depot.

Opposite: Demo in support at St George's Hall, '97.

Winter picket, '97.

Picket next to Gladstone storage tanks.

Above: Mark Steel.

Left above and below: Norse Irish Gate.

Opposite: Demo of support.

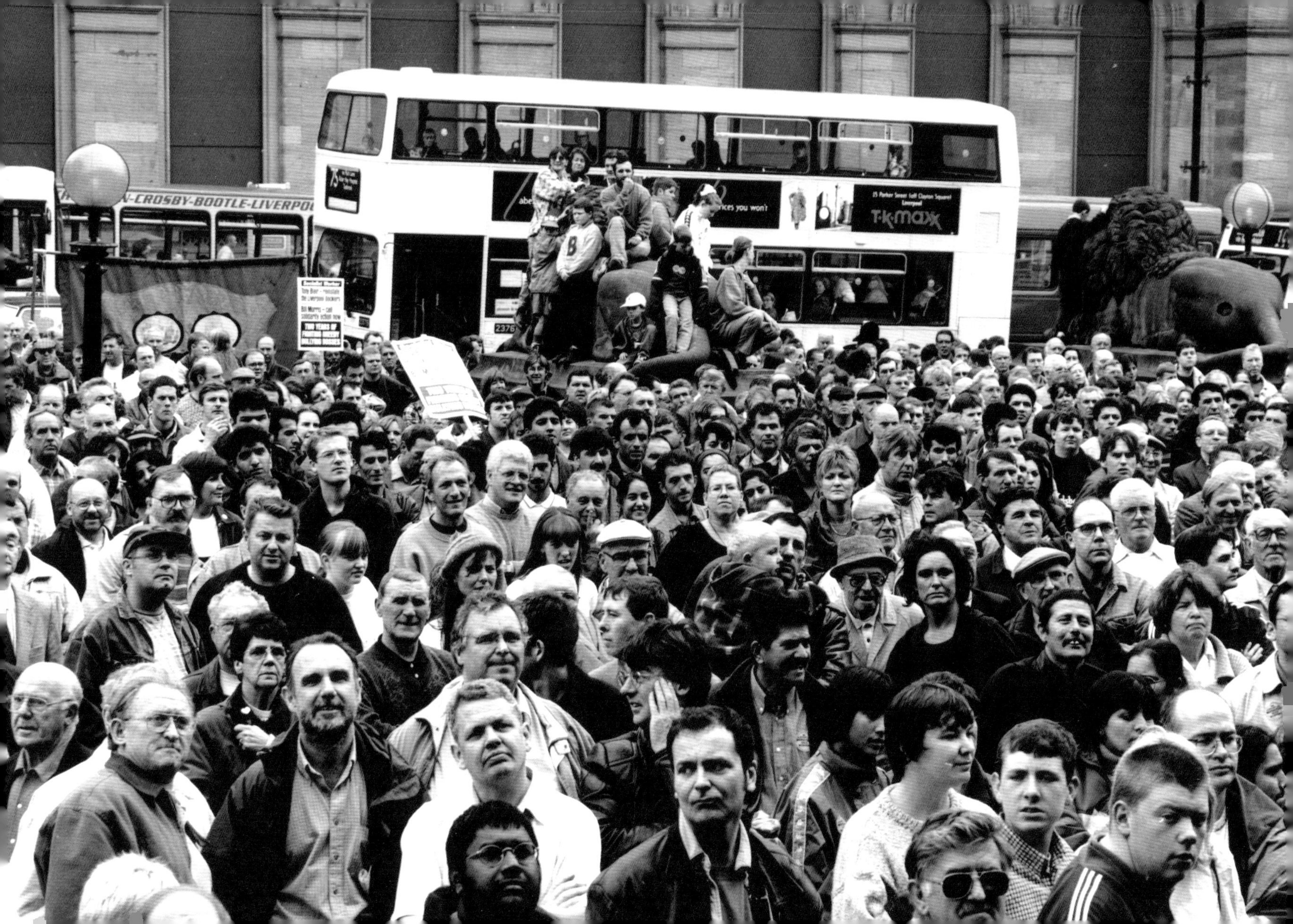
CROSBY-BOOTLE-LIVERPOO
T·K·MAXX

Above left: Father Michael DeFretas of St Joan of Arc church, Bootle.

Above right: Tony Gardner singing to motorway service station staff on the way back from picket of Sheerness in Kent (also owned by MDHC).

Opposite: Frankie Jones and Ritchie Gerard in the Elm House pub on the Dock Road.

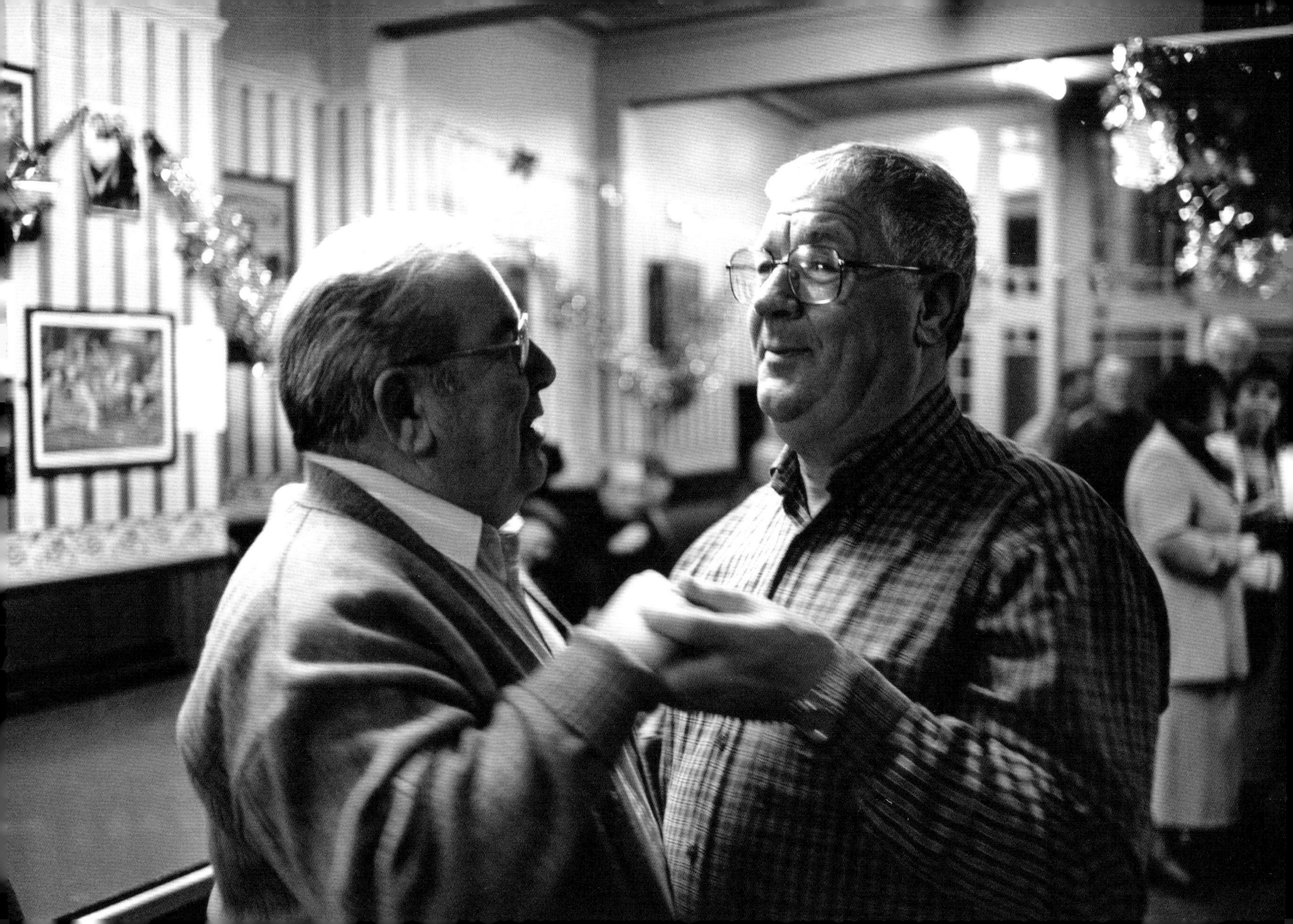

Reclaim the Streets and OSD on Liverpool demo.

Turkish/Kurdish supporters from the Daymar Centre, London come to Liverpool demo in support.

Left: Colin Mitchel and his son Colin help Billy (Kipper) Lynch with his crossword.

Opposite: Alan Haigh, Tony Atkins and Terry Porter.

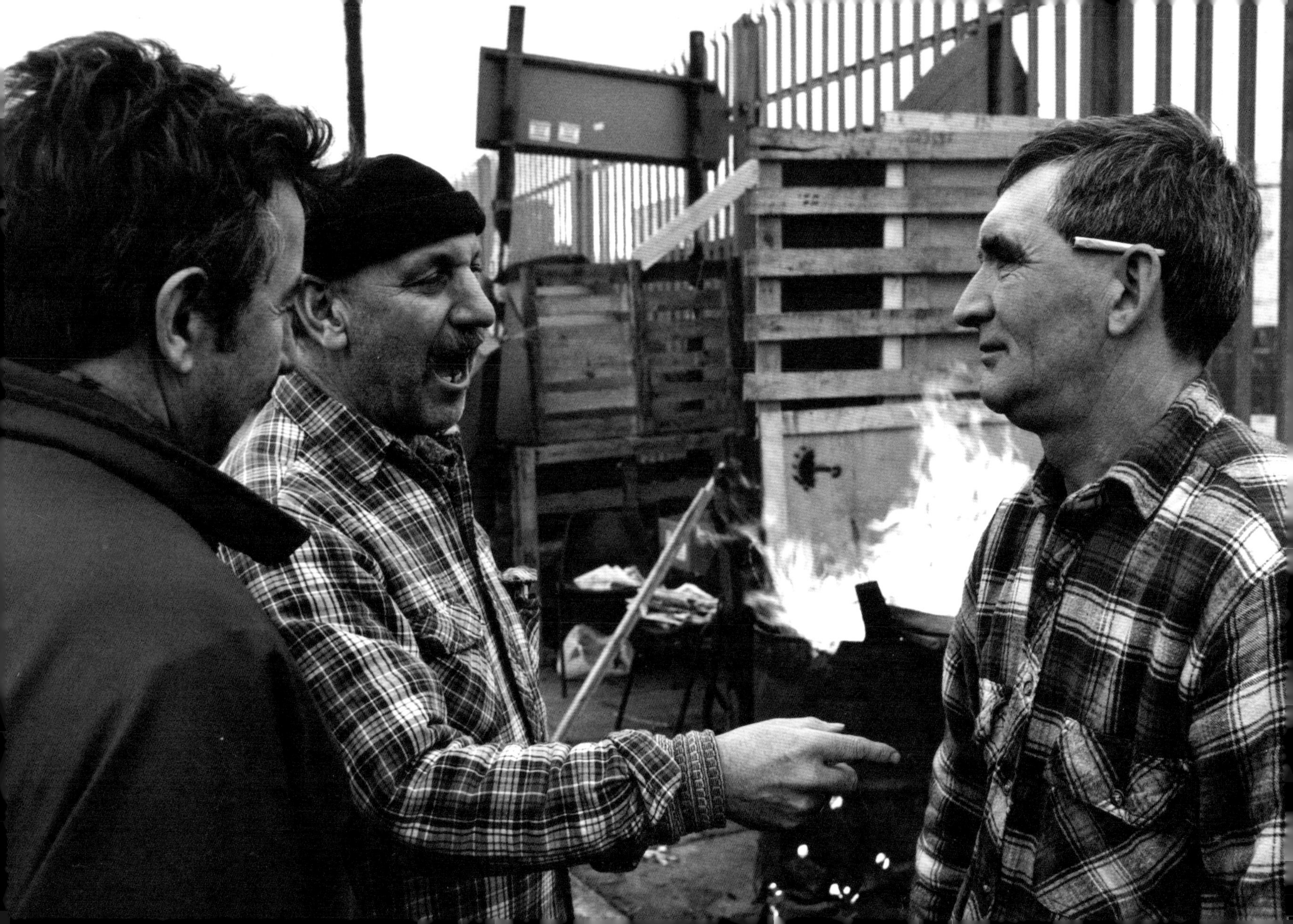

24-hour occupation of Gantry, '97.

Arthur Scargill and ET.

Chris, Tommy and Georgie.

Terry McGuire and Bobby Morrow help Kipper Lynch with his crossword.

The Sheriff watching scabs.

WOW at St Georges Hall rally, '97.

Operational Support Division copper threatens to smash my camera if I took his photo during Town Centre protest in support of the Dockers, '97.

OSD threaten peaceful demo.

Dockers, supporters and Reclaim the Streets occupy MDHC headquarters (the Rat house) '97.

Occupation and protest at Seaforth docks.

Reclaim the Streets wind up coppers during docks occupation.

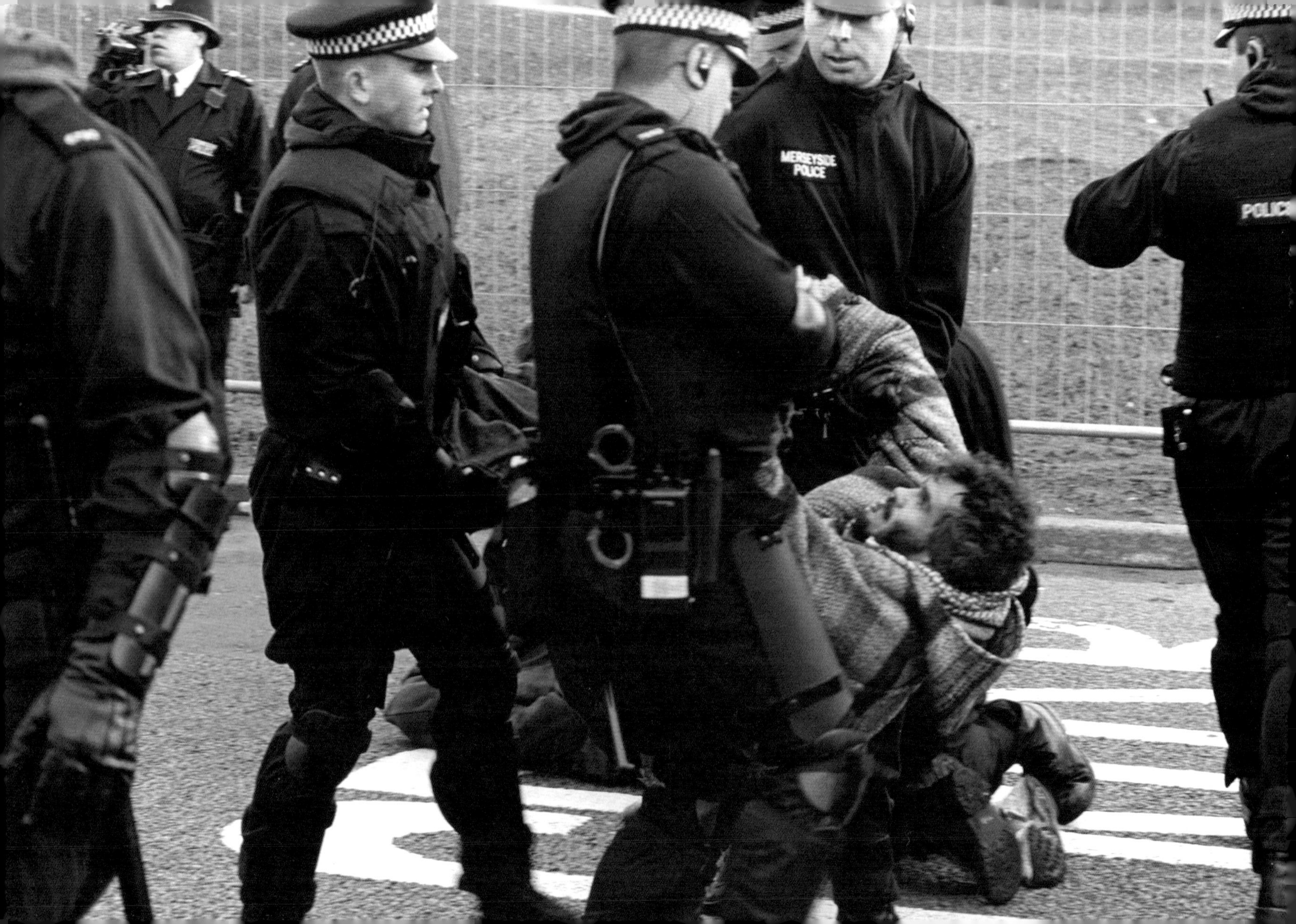
MERSEYSIDE
POLICE

Above: Jimmy Davies Snr arrested during occupation and protest at docks.

Right: Tony Benn.

Opposite: Supporters arrested and beaten during protest.

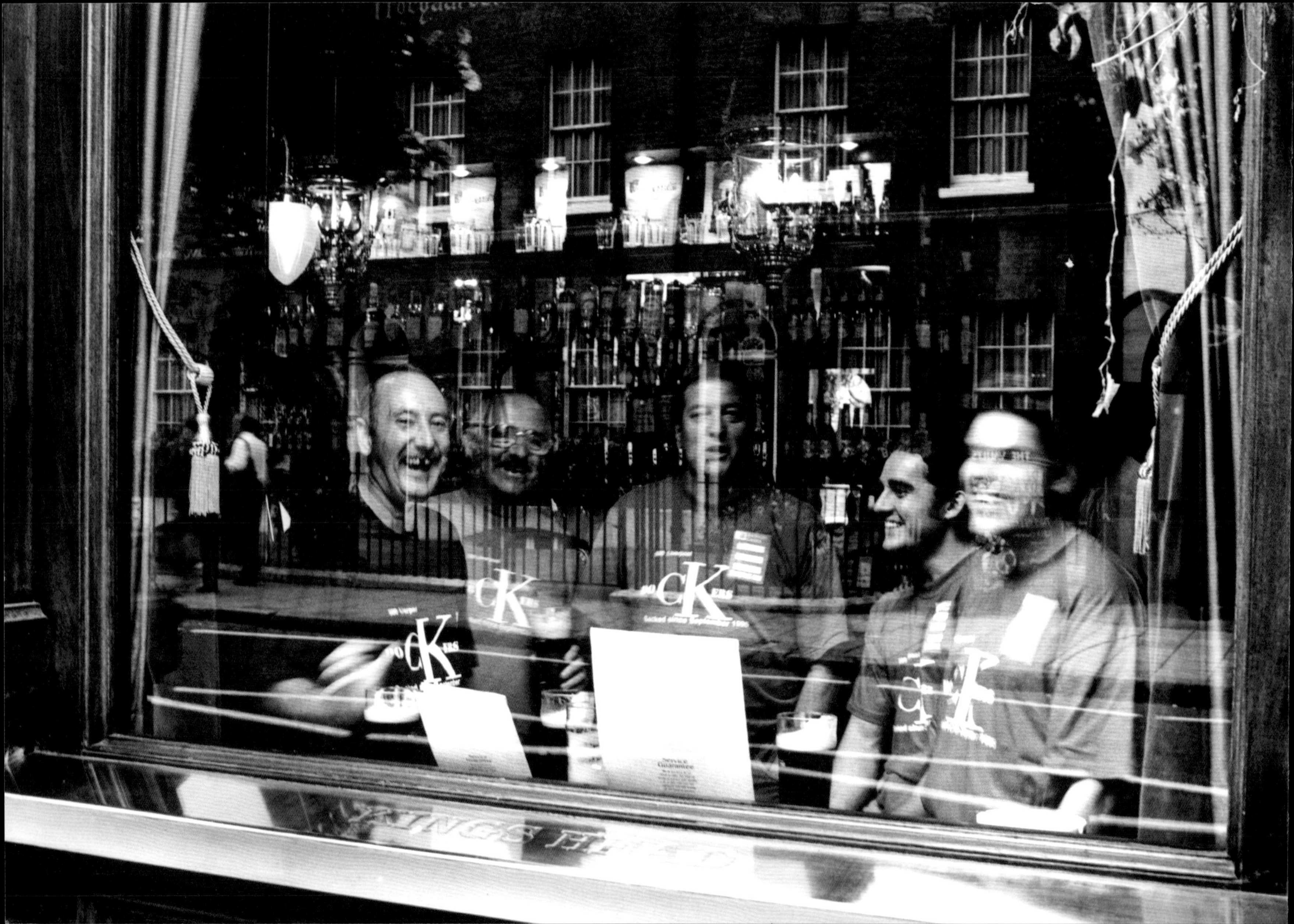

Jimmy Cauty, Jimmy Davies and Bill Drumond.

Opposite: Eddie, Georgie, Tony, Mark and Liam escape to the pub during KLF Barbican event in support of the Dockers.

KLF at the Barbican, London.

Opposite: Joe and Stevie.

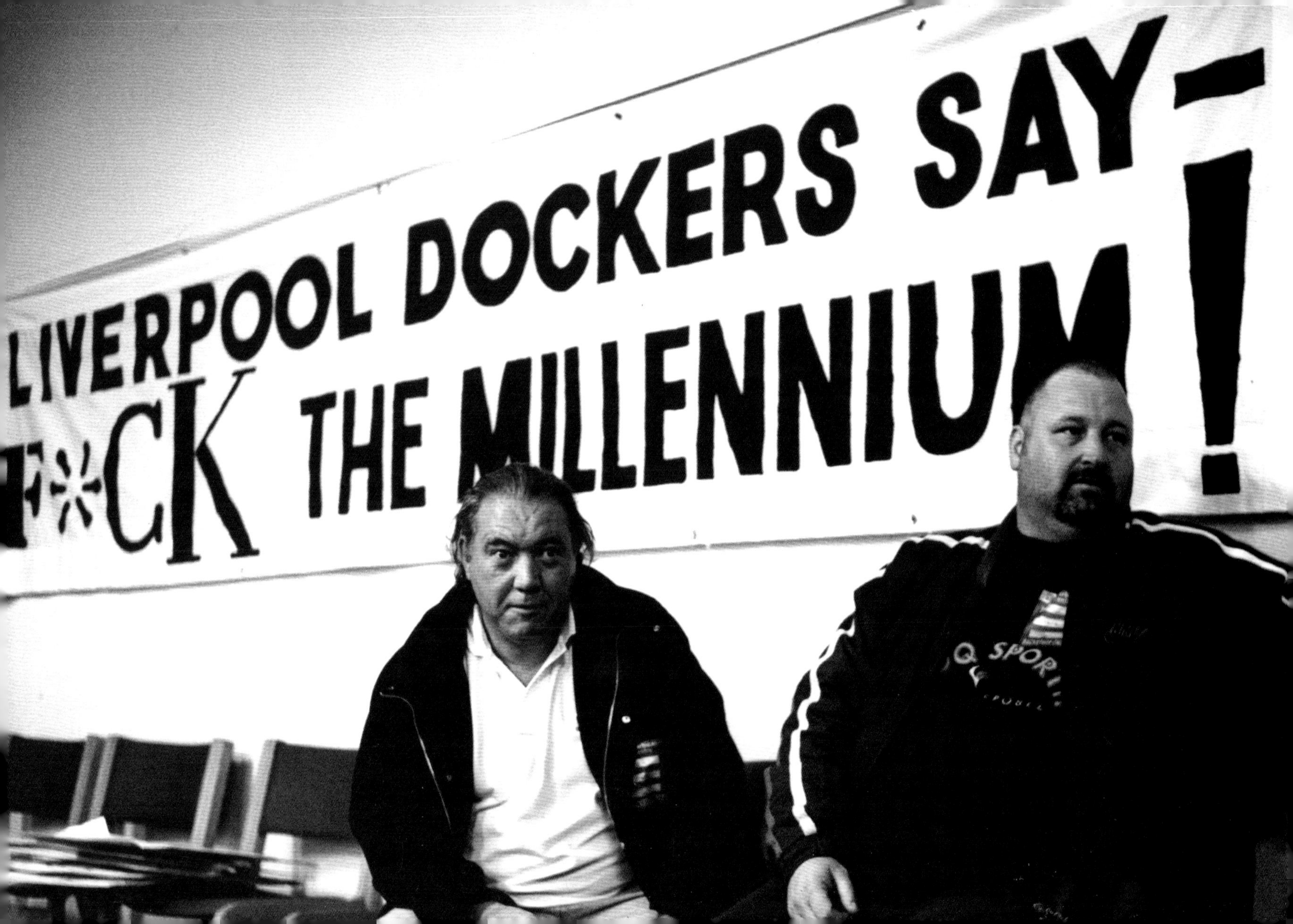
LIVERPOOL DOCKERS SAY –
F*CK THE MILLENNIUM!

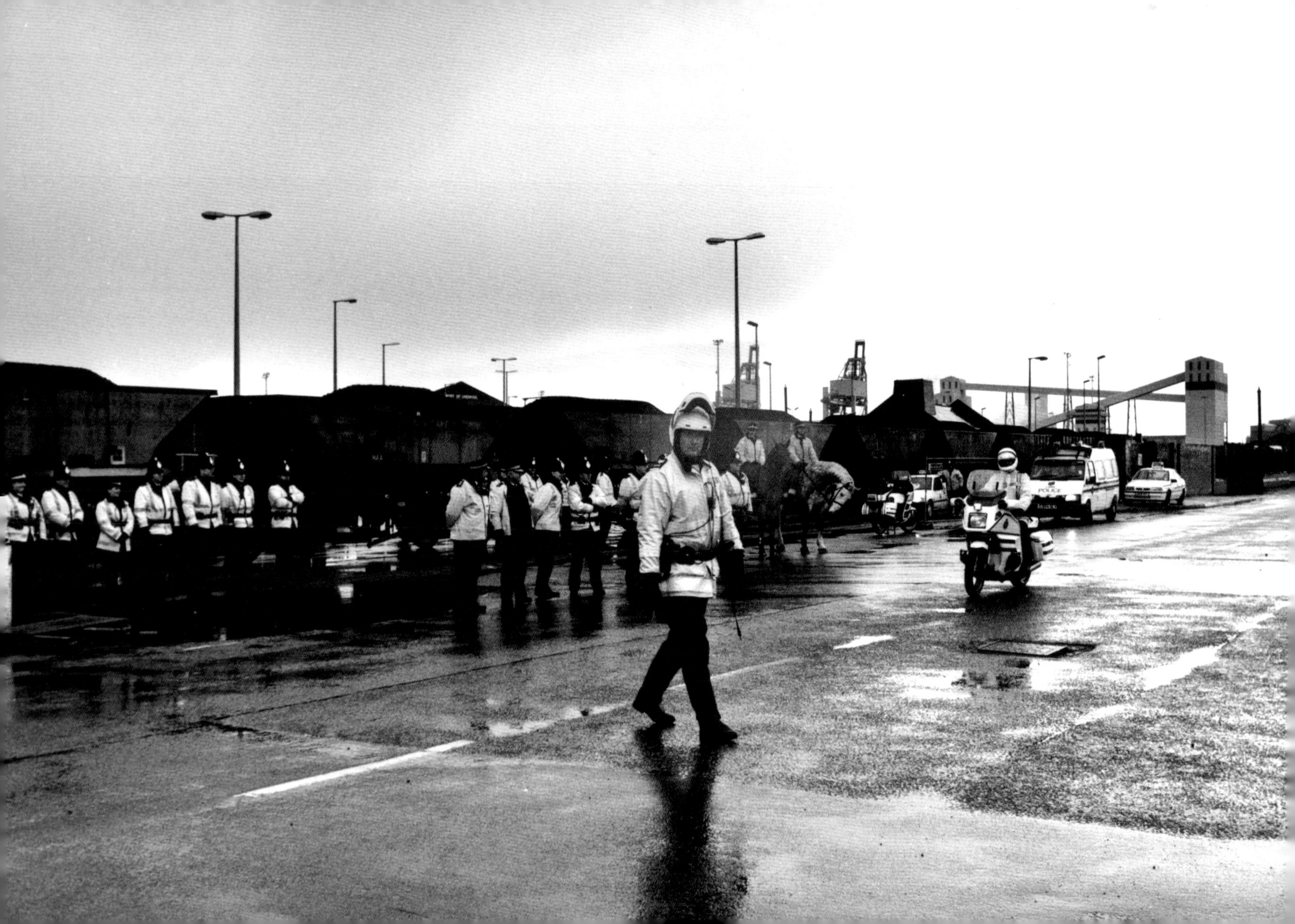
POLICE

Above: Reclaim the Streets and environmentalists at a Dockers' meeting.

Right: Justice demo to Parliament with other groups including the Hillsborough Justice Campaign just prior to the Blair government taking power, '97.

Opposite: Dock Road, '97.

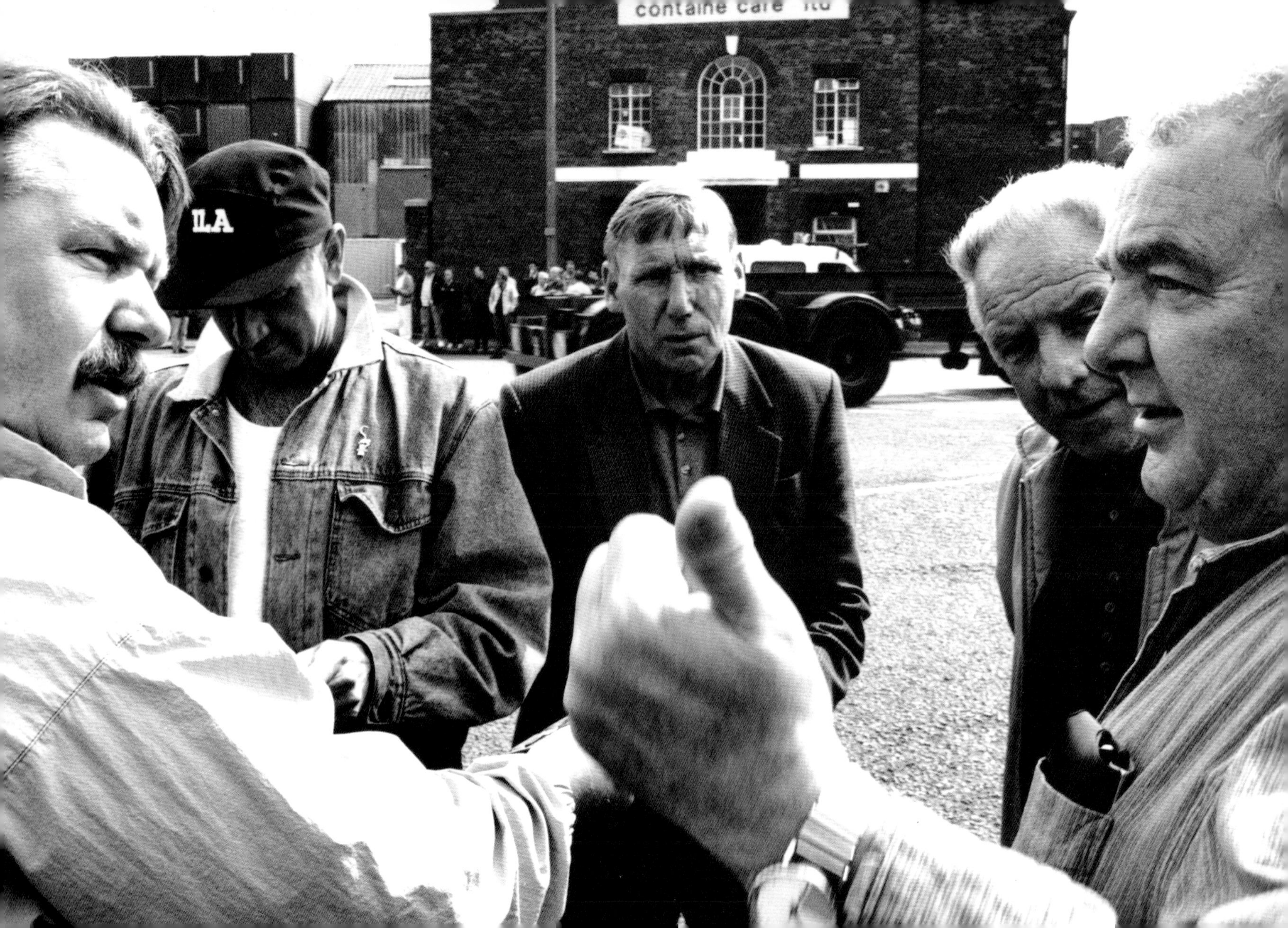
containe care ltd
ILA

Above: Masher.

Below: Seaforth Gate, late '97.

Right: Ricky Tomlinson.

Opposite: Discussion among Dockers, '97.

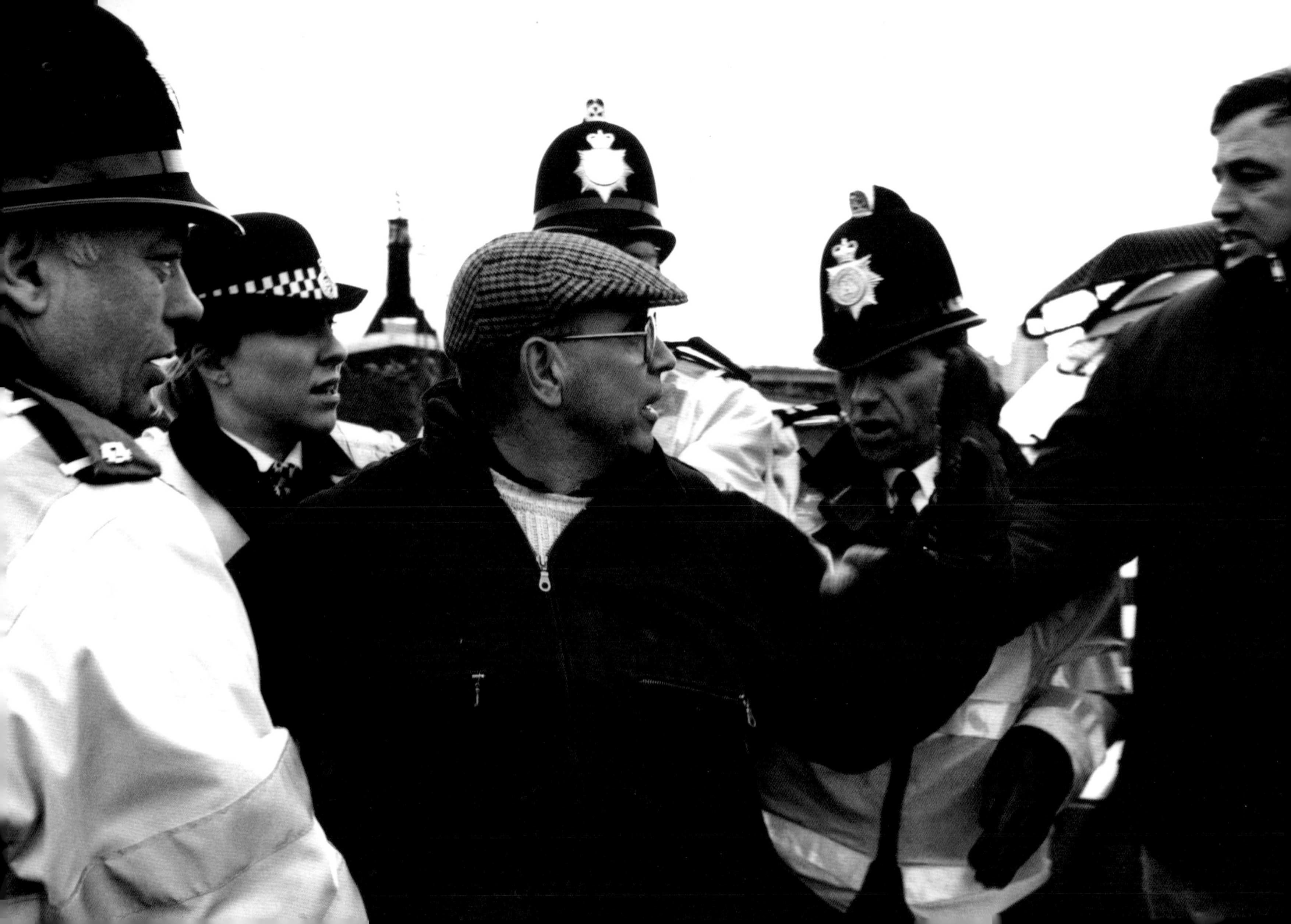

Above: Billy and Jimmy letting scabs know their thoughts.

Above right: Picket hut.

Below right: Making T-shirts.

Opposite: Jimmy arrested at the Seaforth Gate.

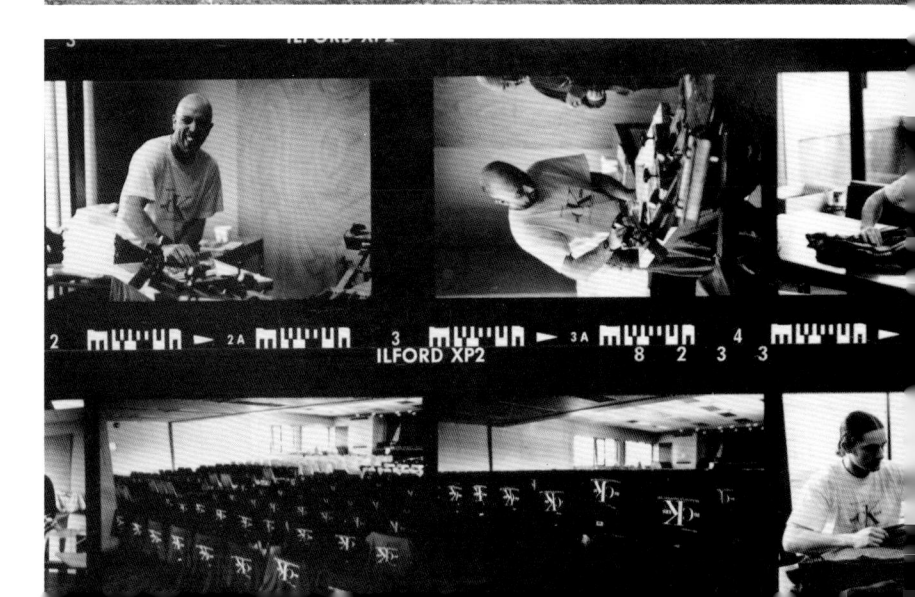

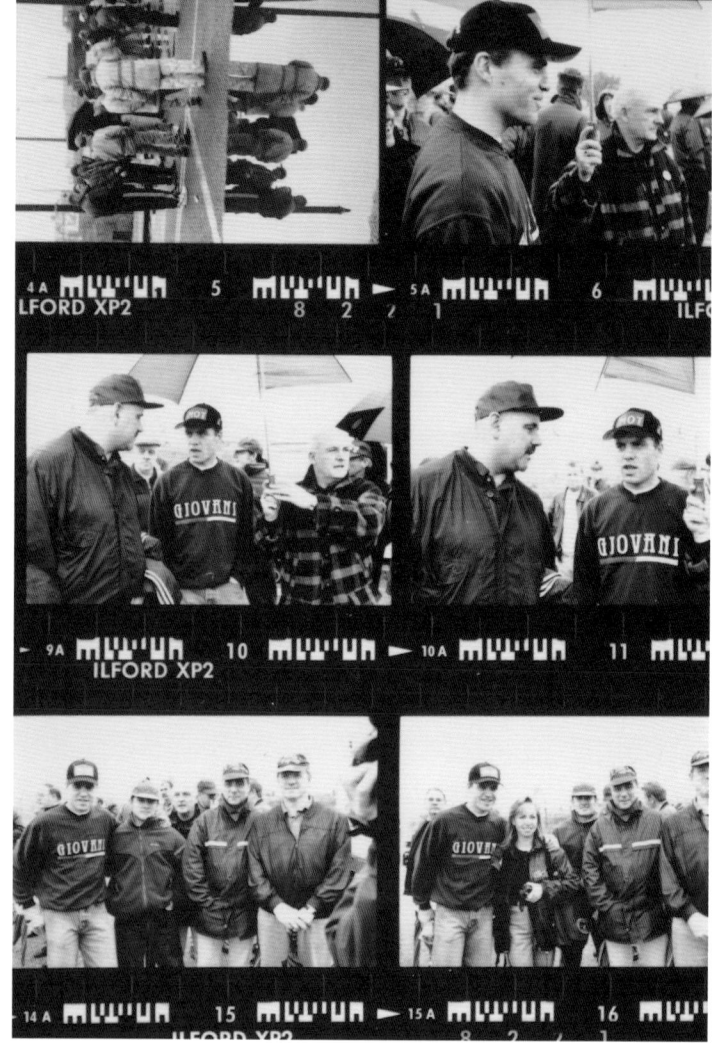

Above: LFC Player.

Left: Peter.

Above: Sheltering from the rain.

Right: Sammy Hopkins.

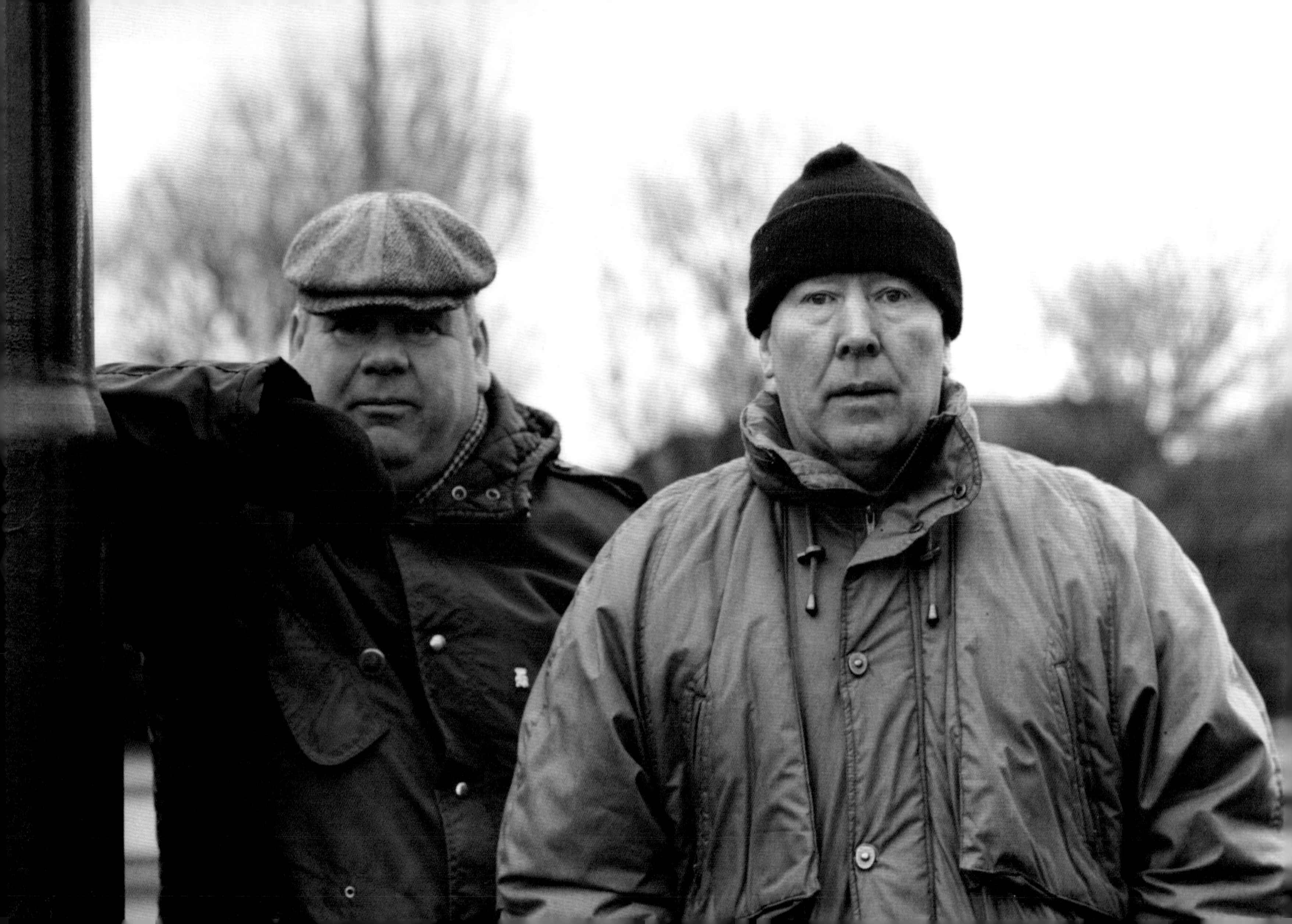

Above: Doreen McNally, Sue Mitchell and Eddie Loydon MP.

Right: Gerry.

Opposite: Joe Ladd and Billy Dunne.

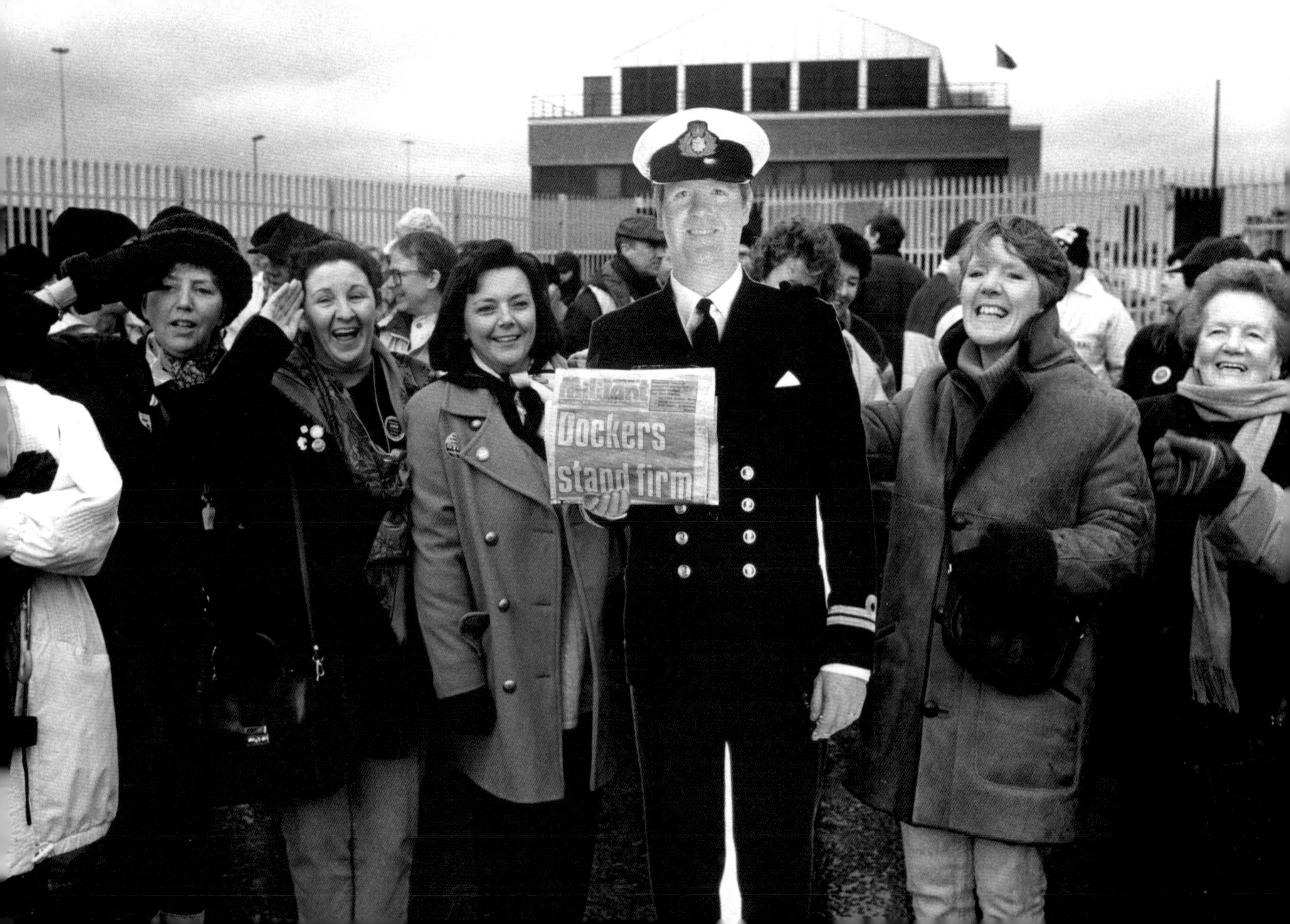
Militant
Dockers stand firm

Above left: Christy and Tommy, Christmas '97.

Above right: Billy 'Kipper' Lynch.

Opposite: The WOW with one of the last issues of *The Militant* being held by 'The Cardboard Captain'. The women found the headline funny because Viagra had just become available.

Below right: Jimmy Davies Snr and Jnr.

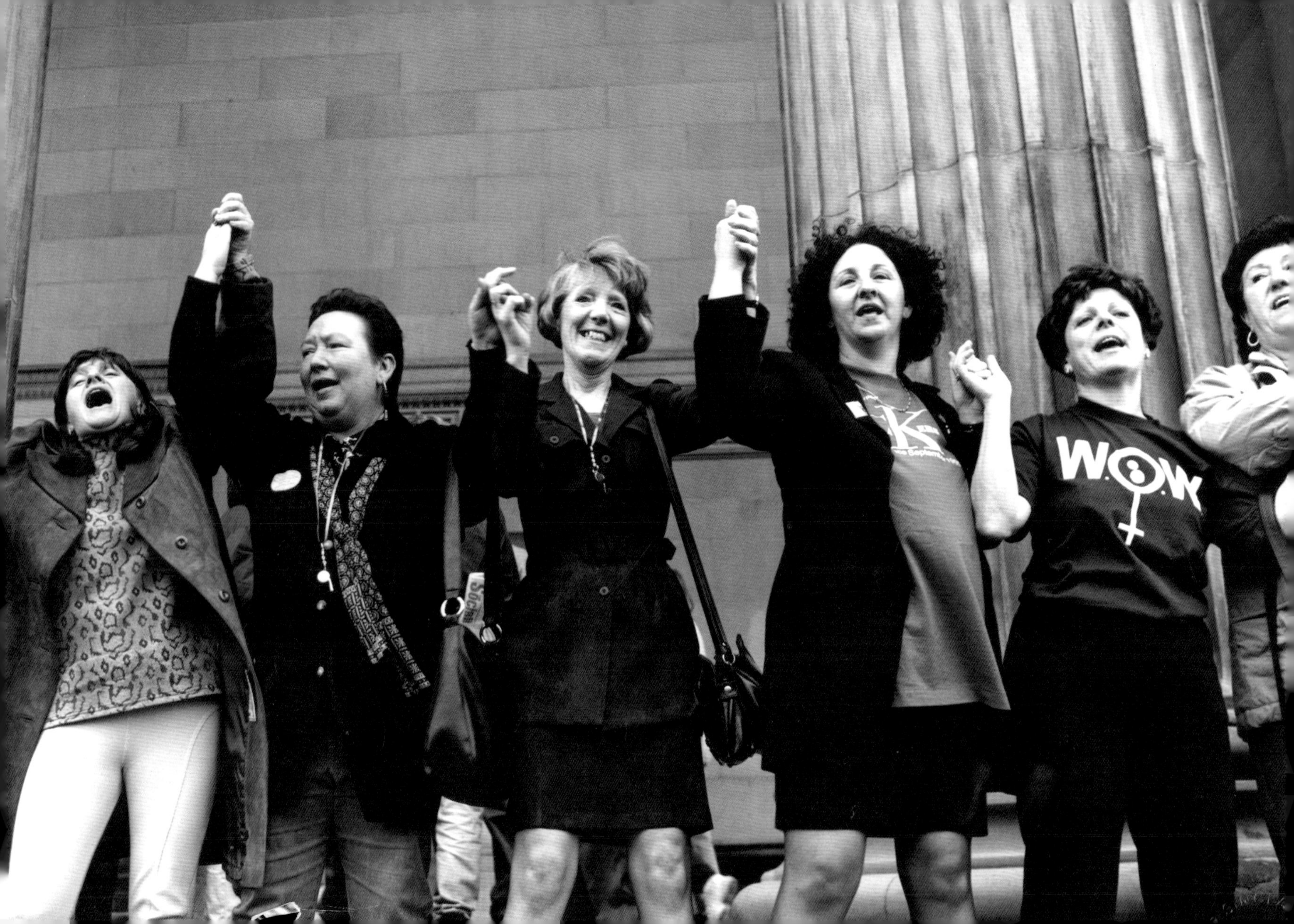
W.O.W.

Above: Dockers' kids.

Right: Lee Hurst.

Opposite: Denise, Anne, Doreen, Sue, Margaret and Winnie singing during Dockers' rally, '97.

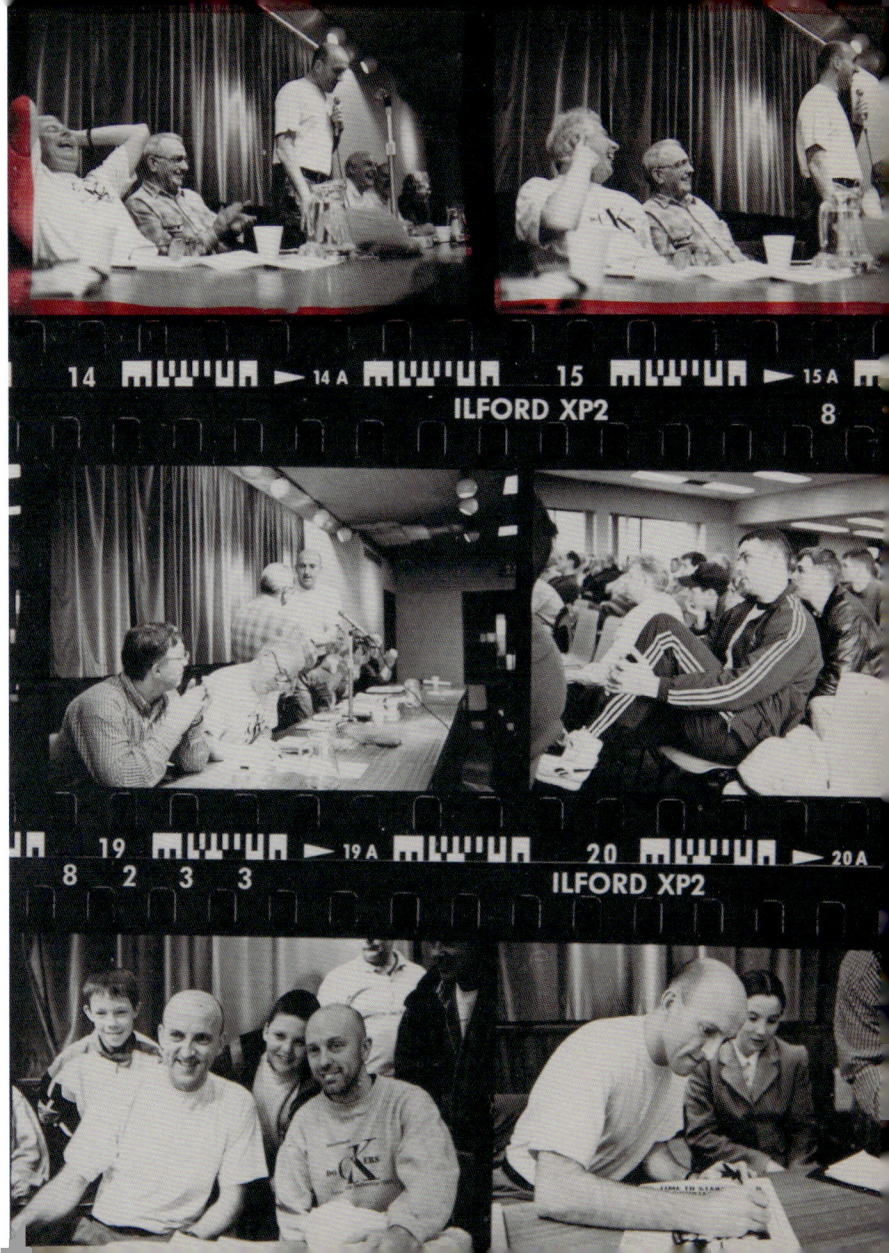

Bobby Hagan, one of the two Boatmen who refused to cross the picket line.

Peter. John.

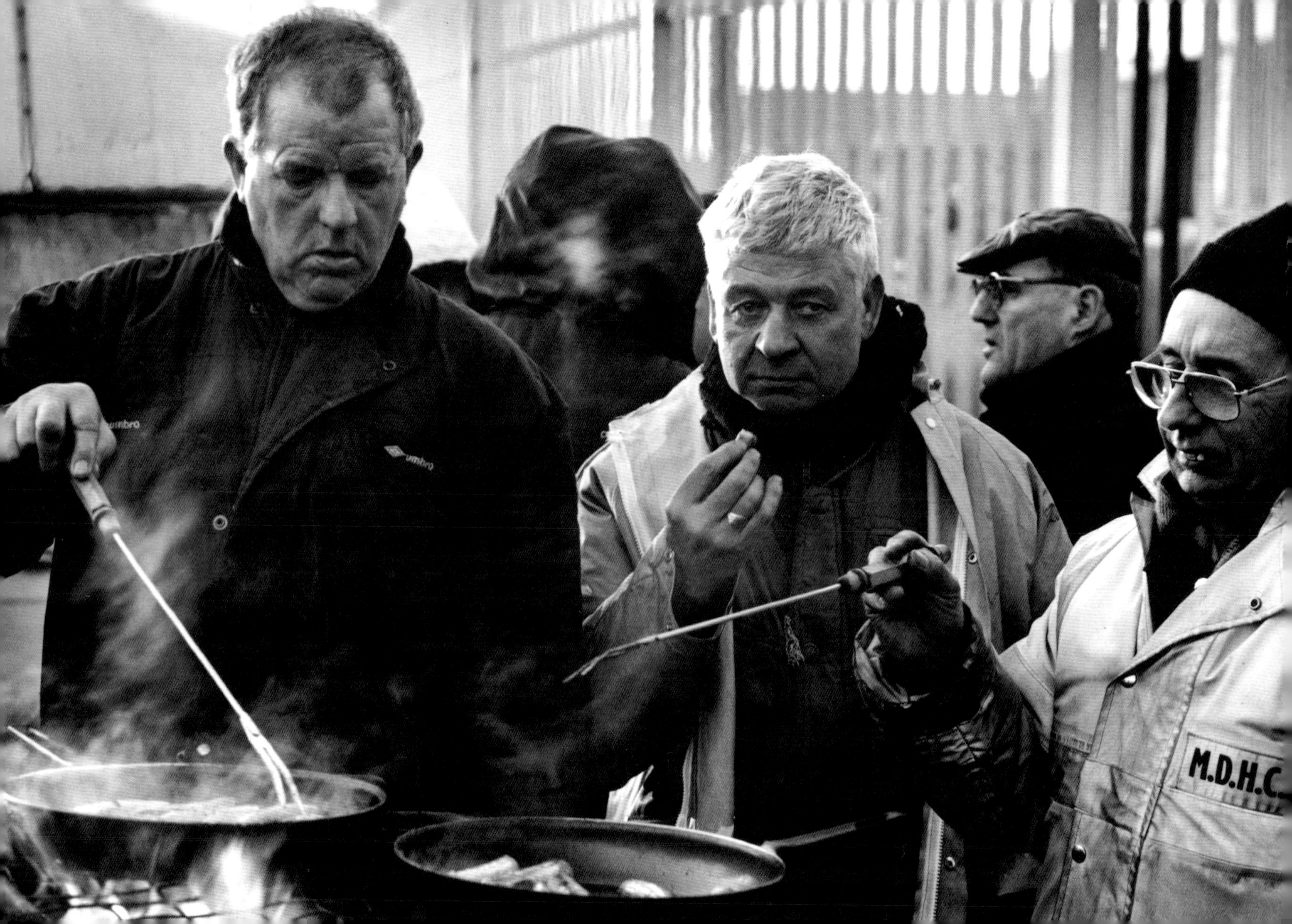
umbro
umbro
M.D.H.C.

Above: Tony Boothe (Tony Blair's father-in-law) and Jimmy Davies.

Right: Tommy Fox.

Opposite: Bozzy, John and Billy.

Jimmy McCumsky's funeral passes the docks, winter '97/'98.

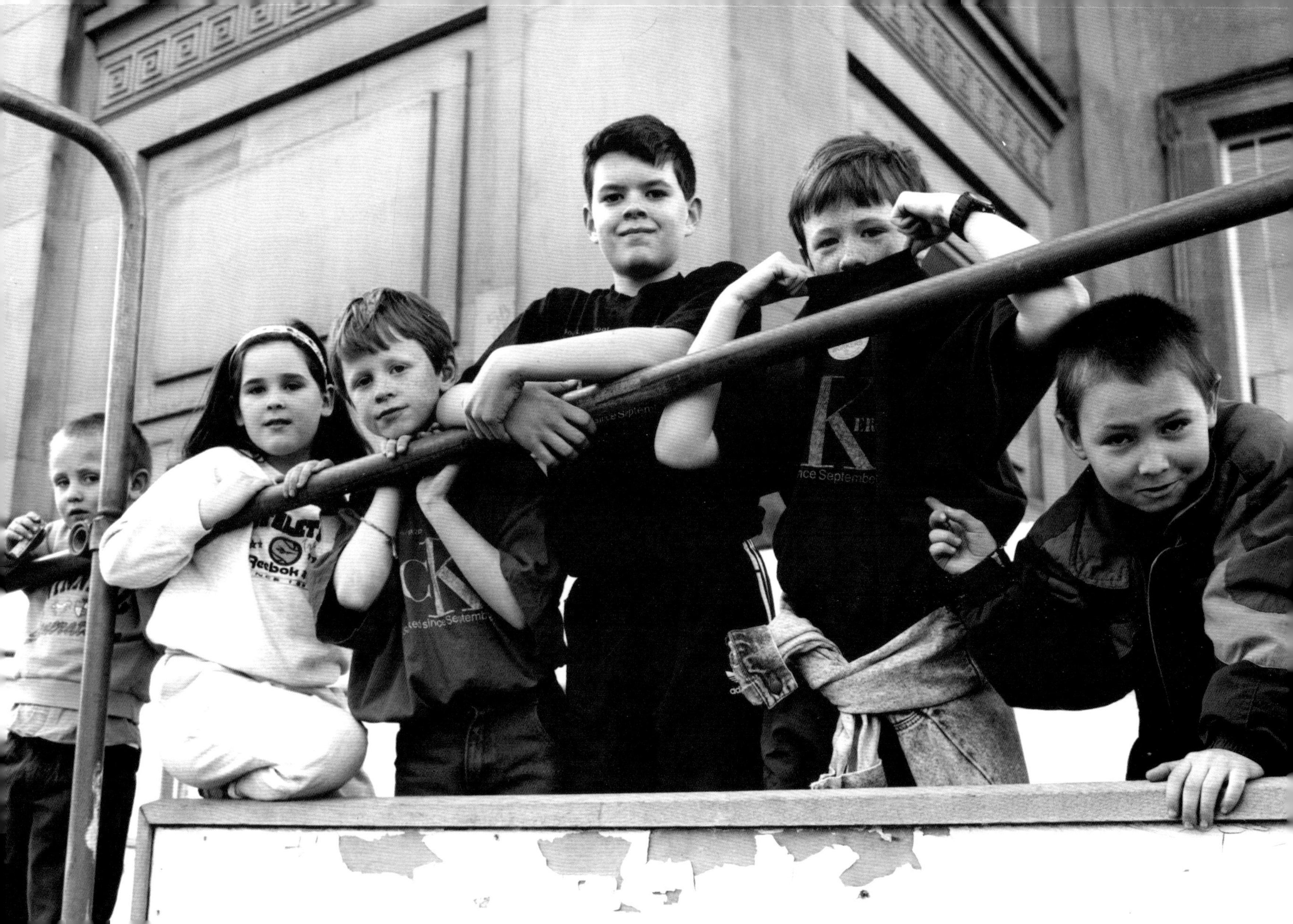

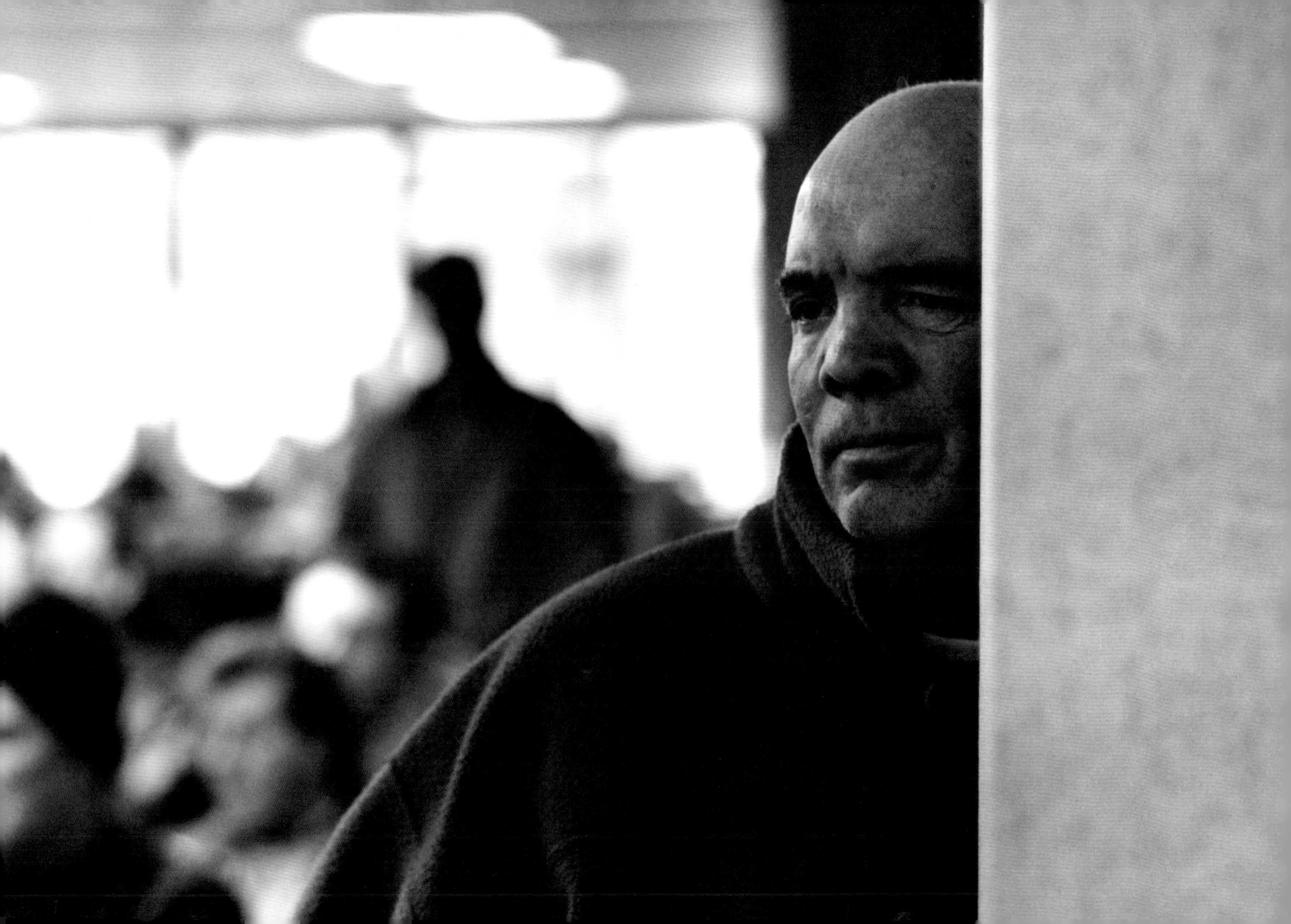

Above: Billy Williams tells a scab his feelings during occupation of Norse Irish ferry with Joe, Chris and Freddy.

Below: Seaforth picket towards end of dispute.

Right: Christmas on picket.

Opposite: Tommy Christy.

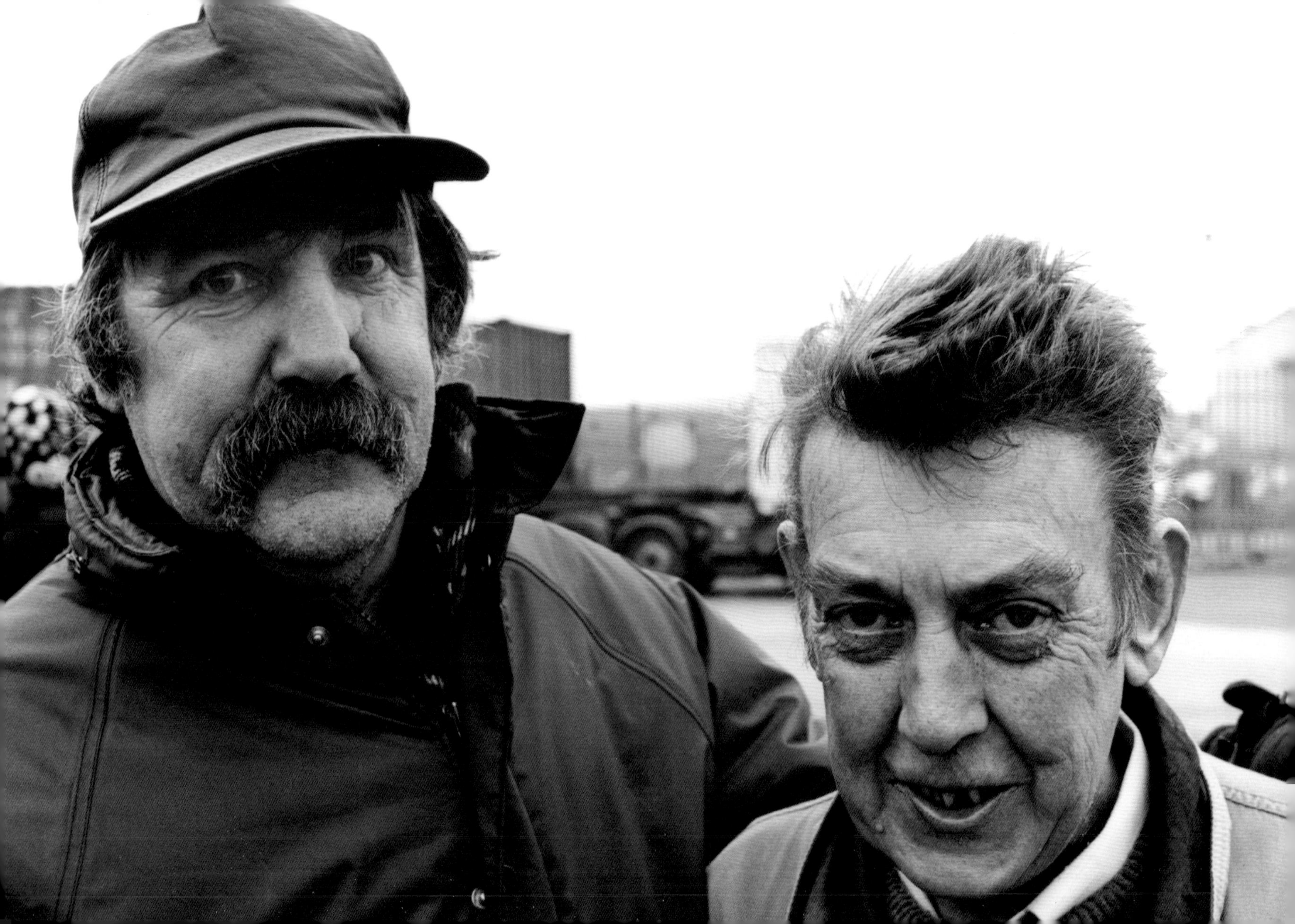

Rose and Kenny at Snowy's funeral.

Opposite: The Sheriff and Snowy.

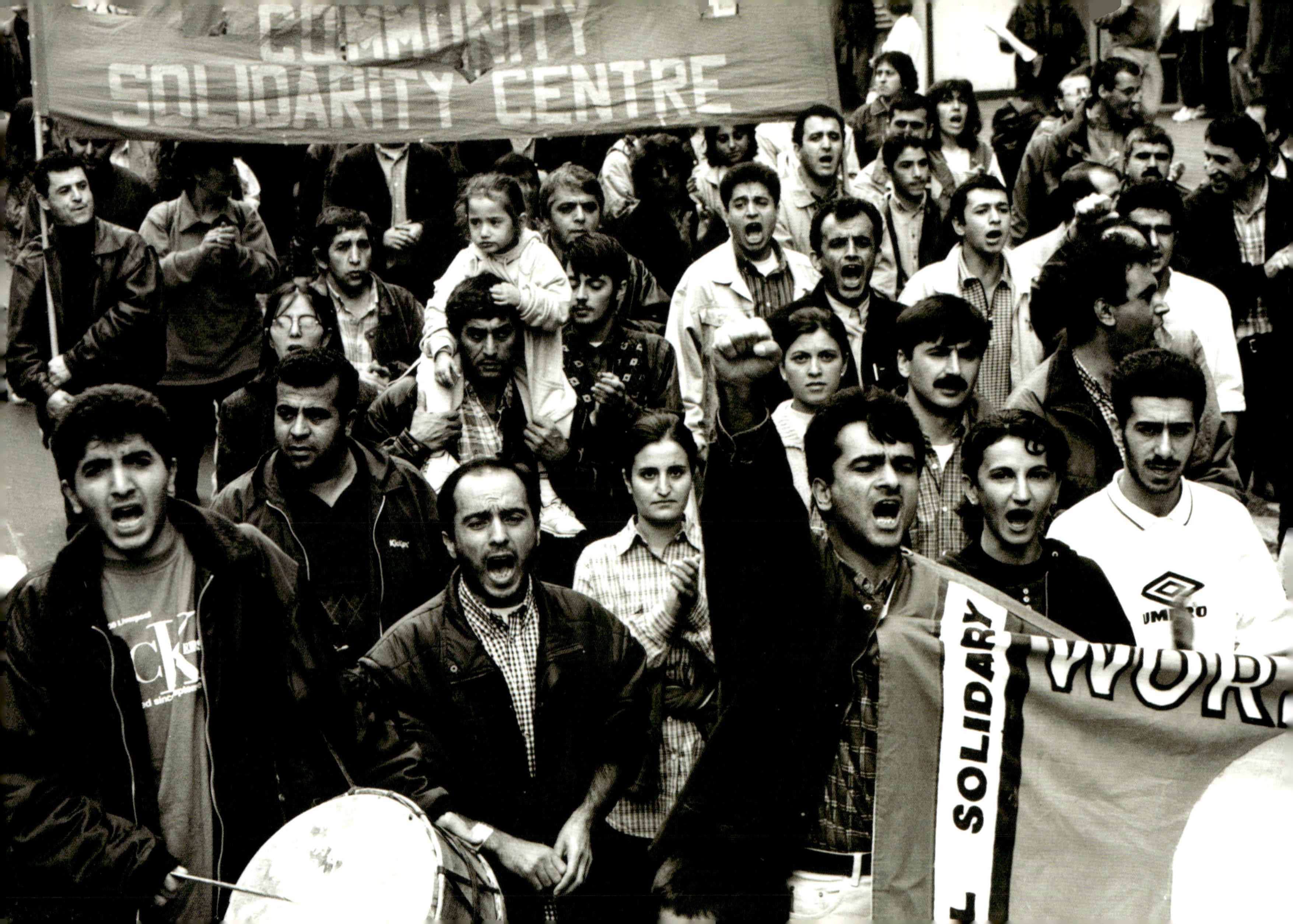
COMMUNITY
SOLIDARITY CENTRE
SOLIDARY
WOR

Above: Watching the horses in Cheltenham while supporting reinstatement of unions at GCHQ.

Right: International delegate with Tony Nelson.

Opposite: Turkish Kurds on demo of support, '97.

John McCabe in Cheltenham for GCHQ rally.

Tucker on his fiftieth birthday.

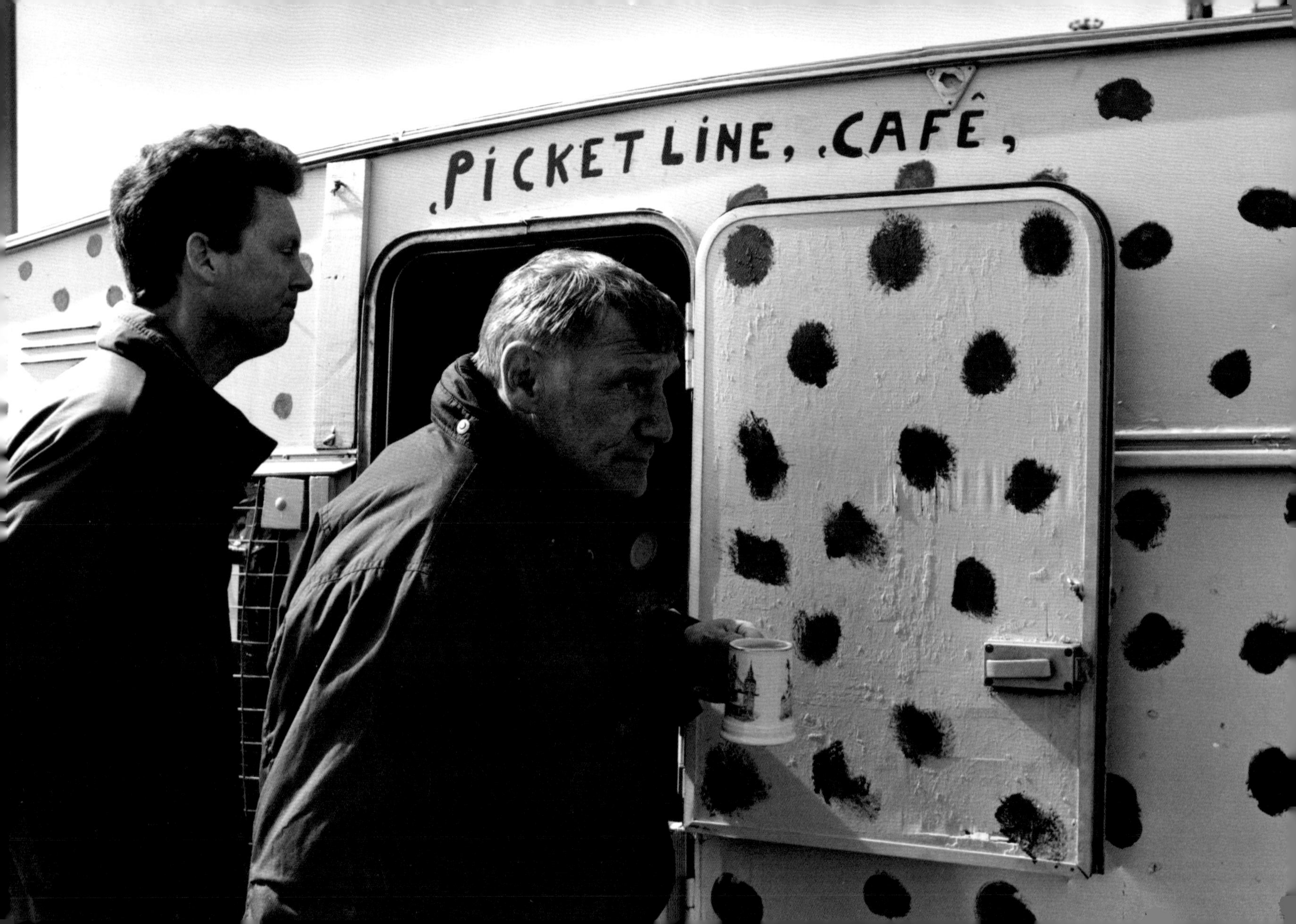
PICKETLINE, CAFÊ,

Above left: Tony Nelson, Kevin Hillsborough and Billy Jenkins, '97.

Above right: Seaforth '97.

Opposite: Colin Curran and Peter Stroud. The Picket Line Café was painted pink with red dots in honour of a Grand National winning horse.

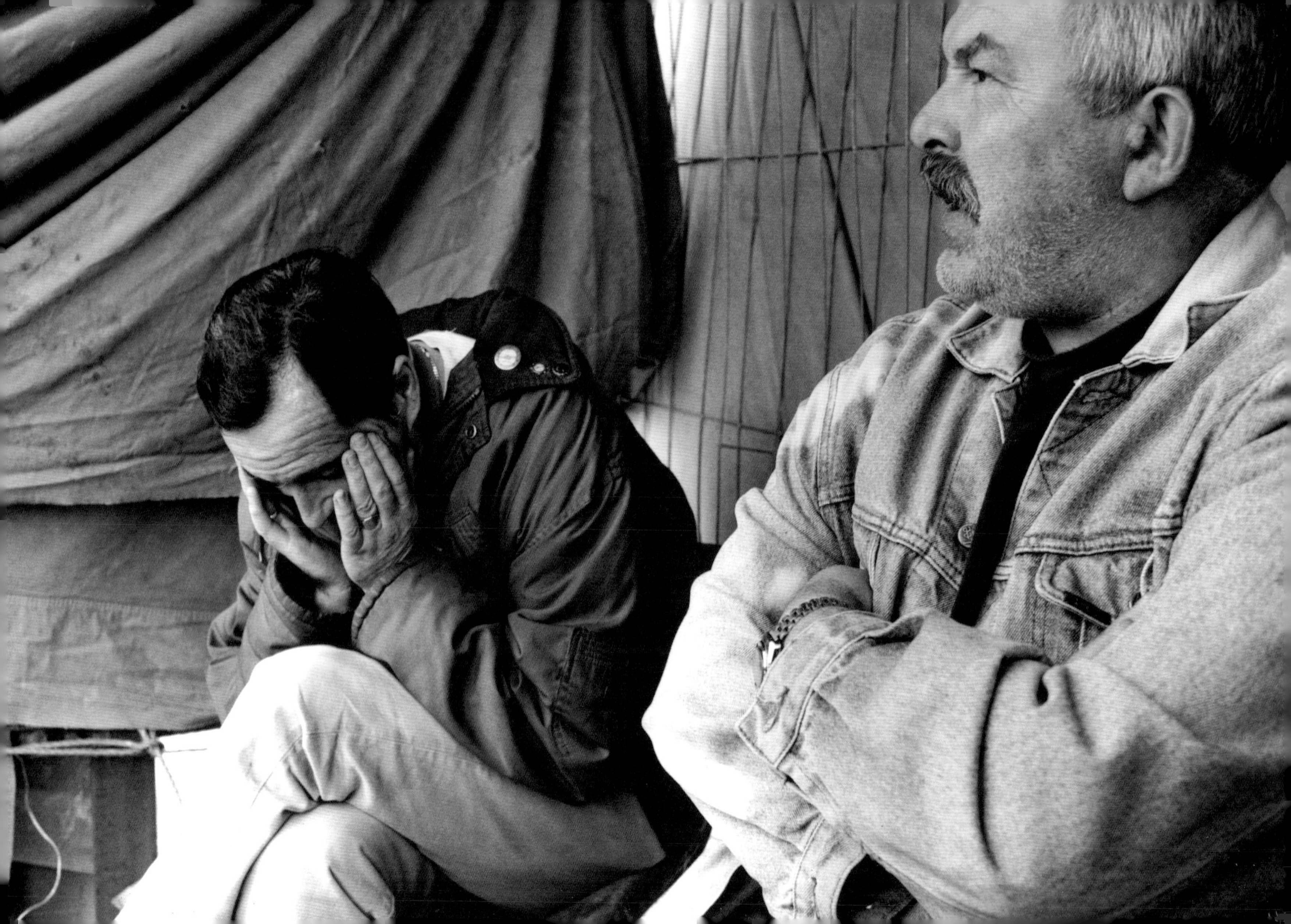

Above and *below right*: Jack Heyman leader of the ILWU, West Coast USA Dockers' leader.

Above right: Leader of Japanese rail workers' union.

Opposite: Peter Barrett and Jimmy Singleton, winter '97.

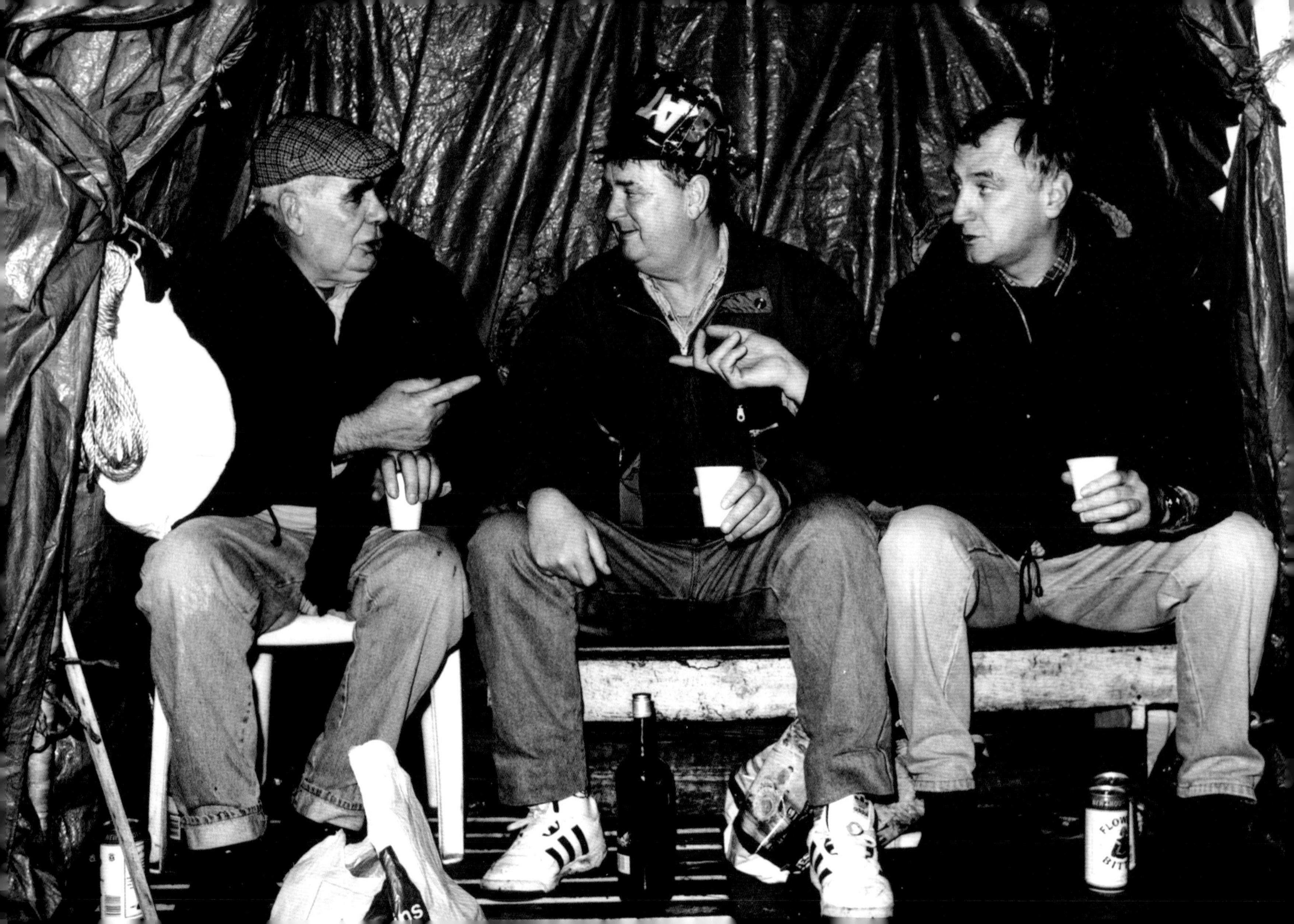

Above: Japanese rail workers.

Below right: Rob Newman.

Opposite: Brownie, Jacko and Jimmy, winter '97/'98.

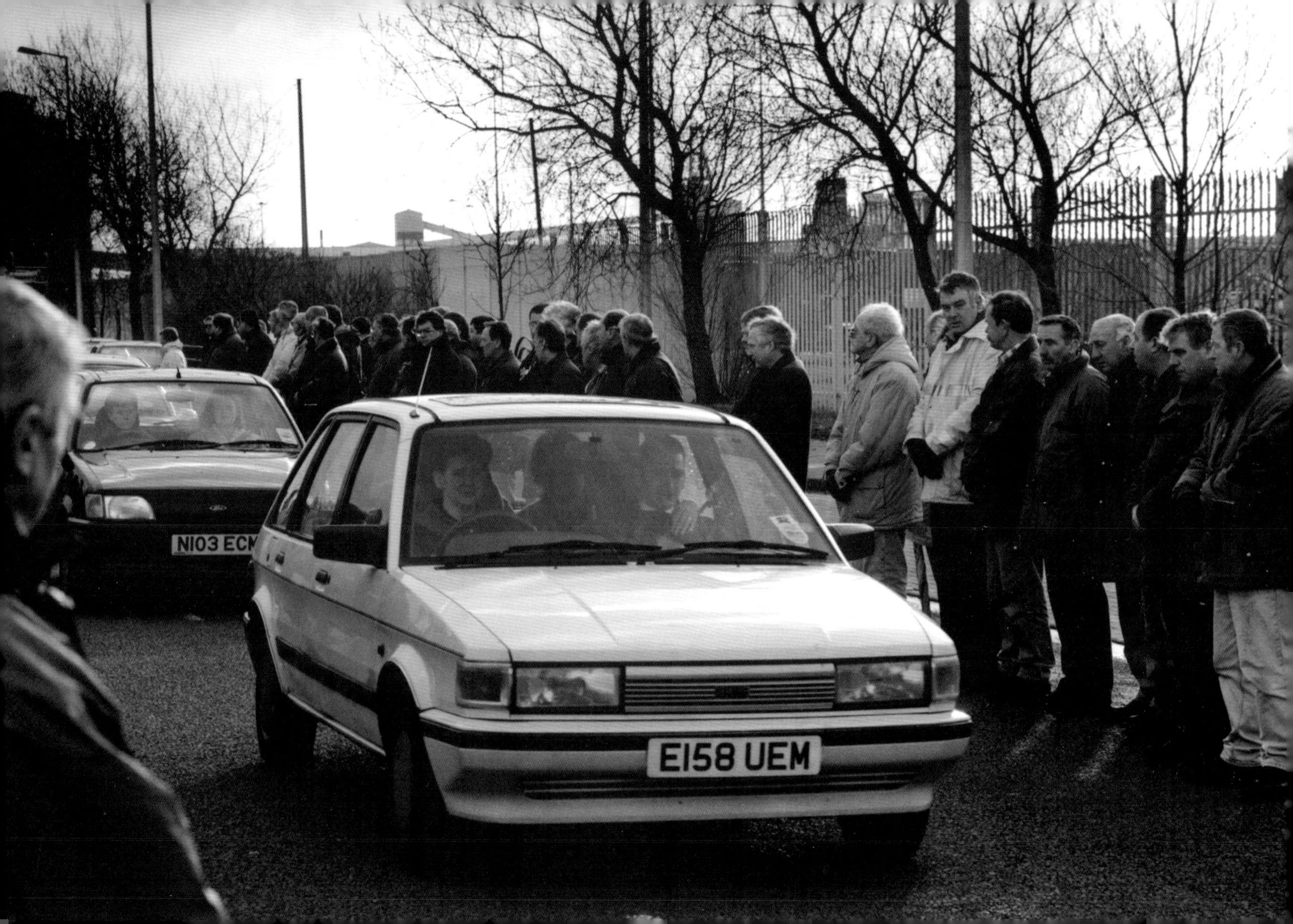
N103 ECM
E158 UEM

Above: Funeral.

Above right: Nick Silvano at Jimmy McCumsky's funeral.

Opposite: Funeral passes docks.

Above: WOW.

Left: Jimmy Nolan speaking at T&G Biennial delegate meeting.

Above: International delegates join march along Dock Road.

Right: Scab watching.

Seaforth, '97.

Protest during T&G BDM in Brighton.

Christmas in the Elm House, '97.

Mary Pendleton and Sue Mitchell, '98.

Caryn Mathews gives benefit advice towards the end of the dispute, '98.

Scottish Miners visit Dockers to talk about '84/85 dispute.

MERSEYSIDE DOCK LABOURERS
T & G
SHOP STEWARDS' COMMITTEE
LIVERPOOL
In
SUPPORT DOCKERS
Socialist Worker
STOP THE GREEDY BOSSES!
SUPPORT THE STRIKES
Tell our union leaders to fight

Larry.

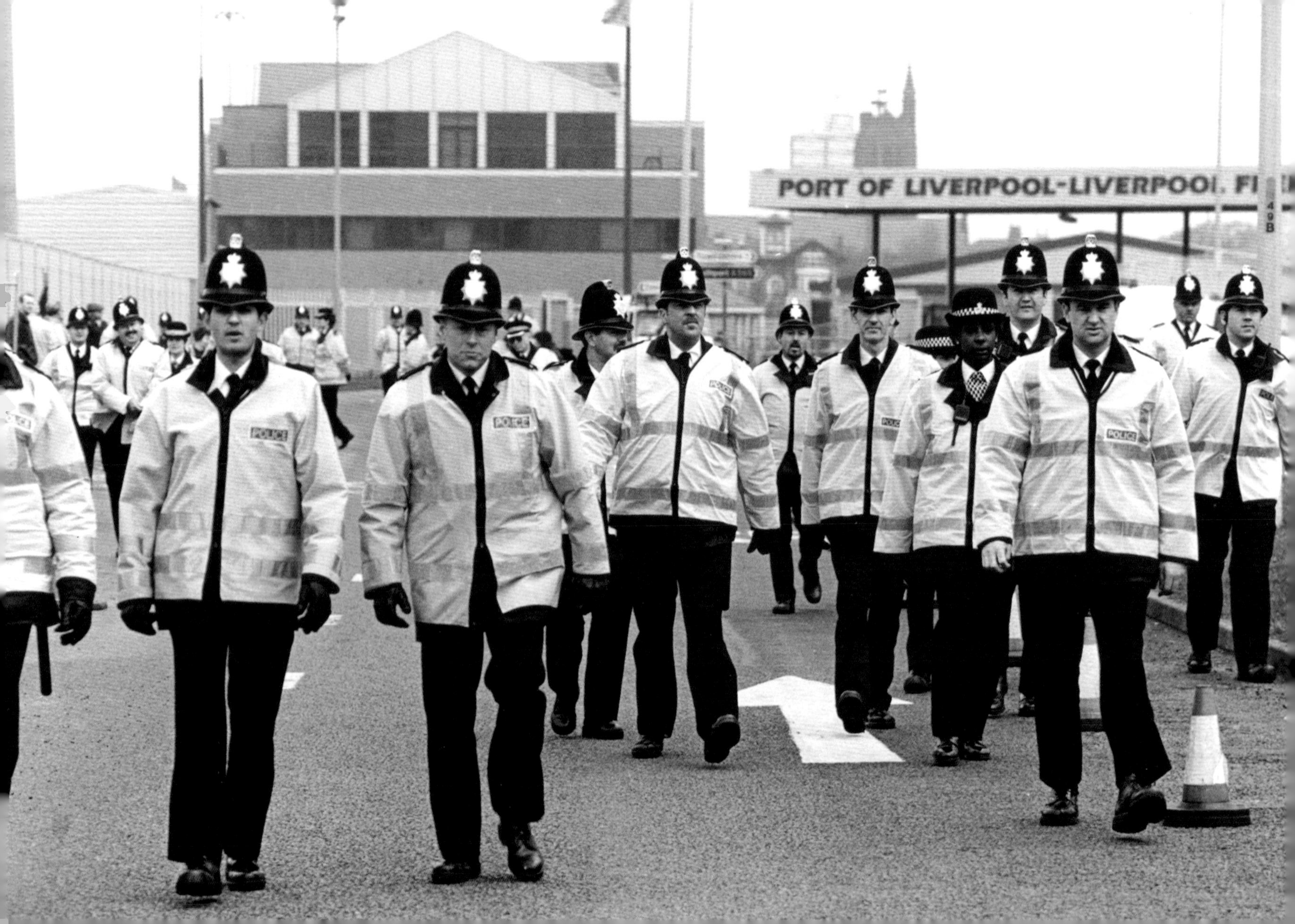
PORT OF LIVERPOOL-LIVERPOOL
POLICE
49B

Above right: Coppers in Sheerness video Liverpool Dockers.

Opposite: Coppers at Seaforth.

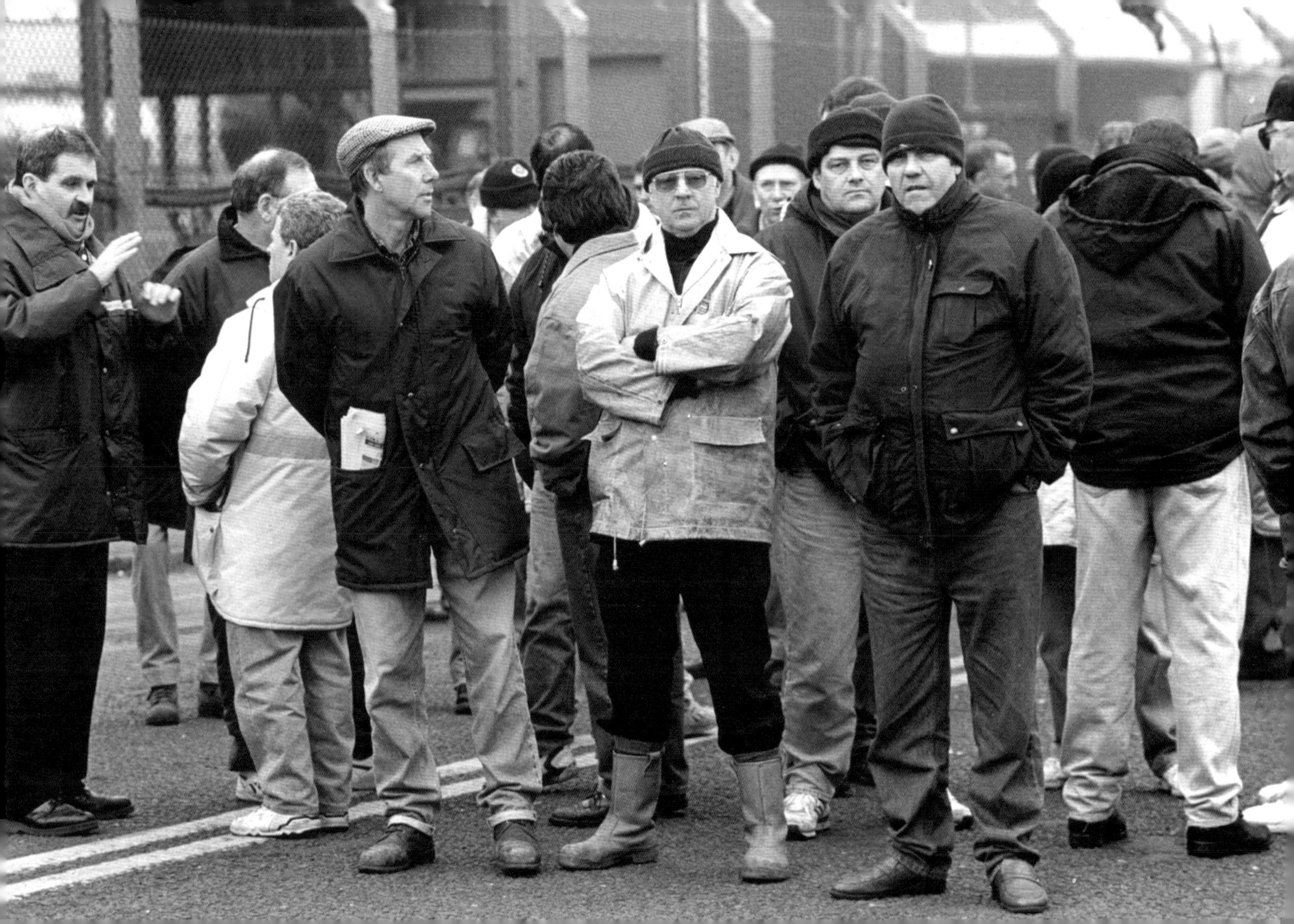

Above: Coach back from Sheerness.

Above right: Terry, Mark and John.

Below right: Peter Clee.

Opposite: Grain Terminal.

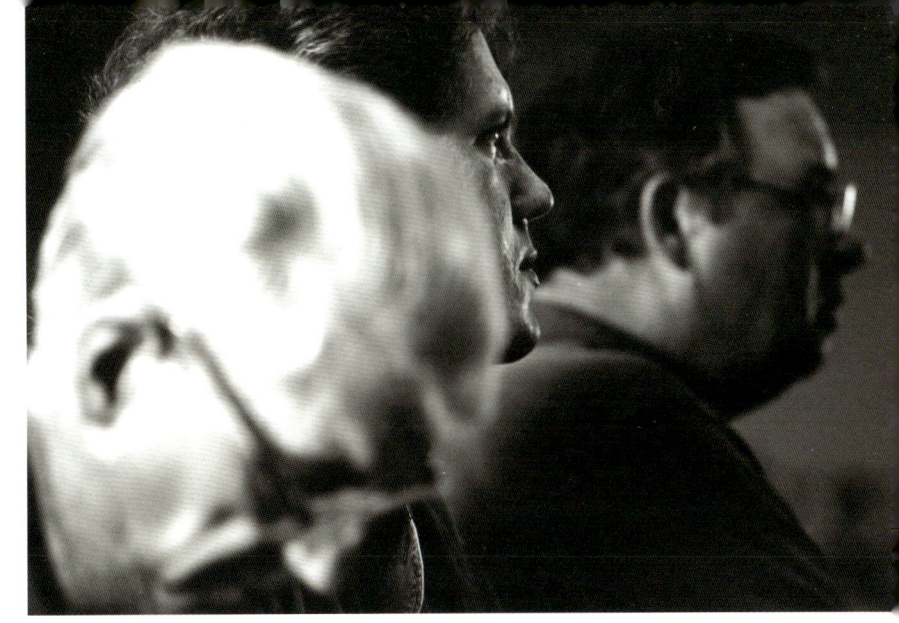

Above: Jimmy and Michel Murray from Canada.

Opposite: Peter Wharton, the Boatman.

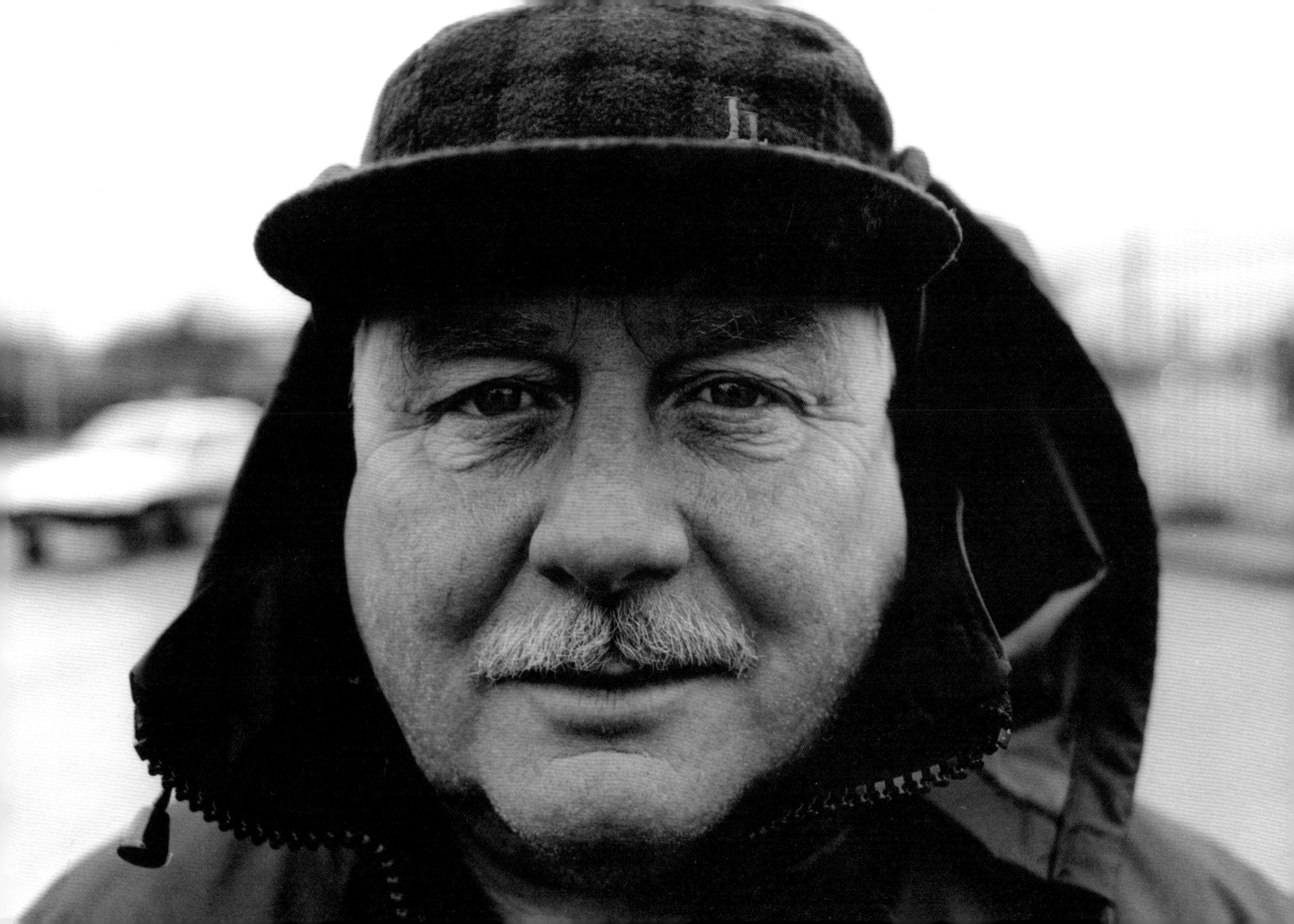

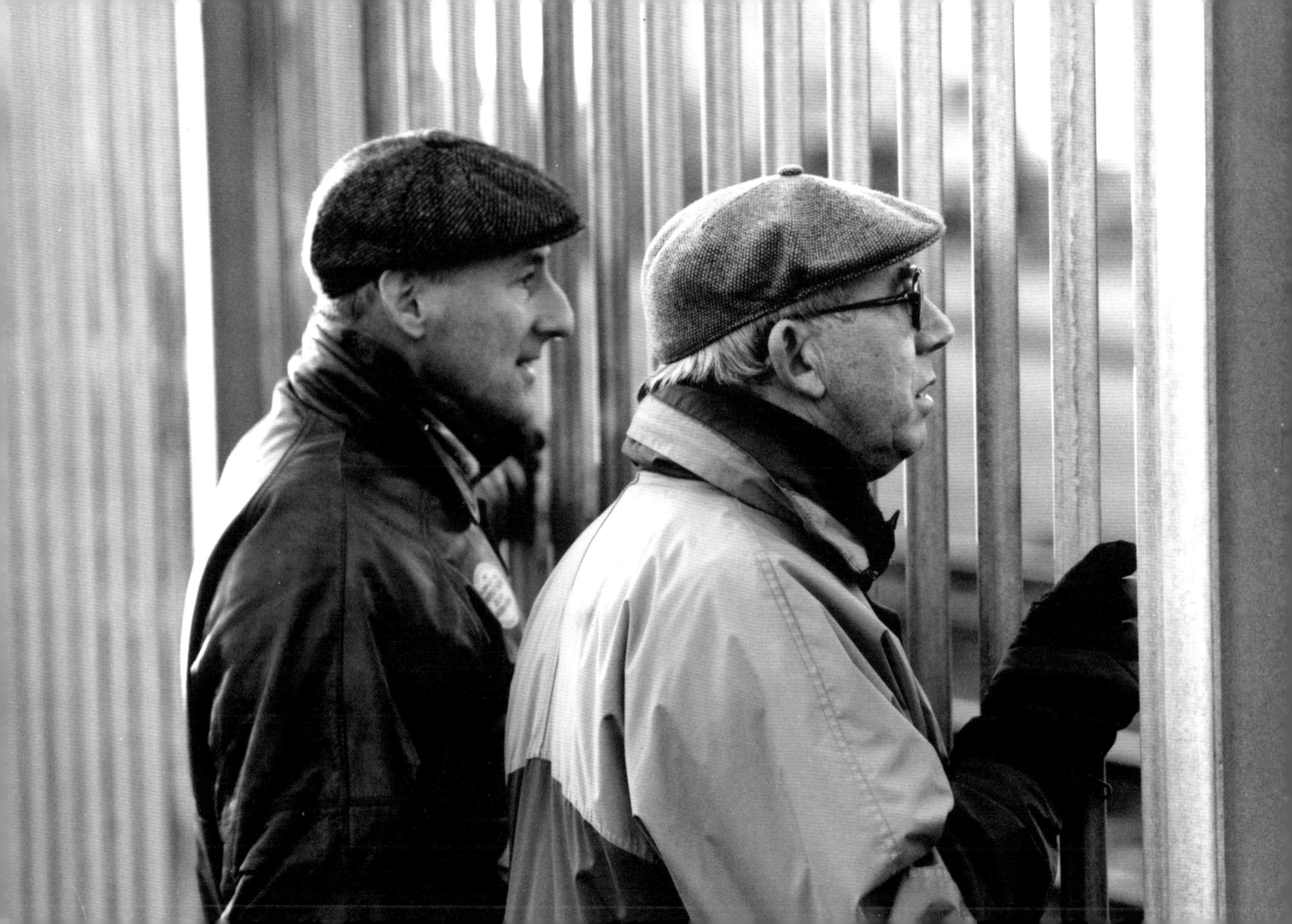

Above left and right: WOW at end of the dispute.

Opposite: Stan Phillips and Terry Barrett. Last days of watching scabs, '98.

Above: WOW meeting near the end.

Opposite: Billy serving tea.

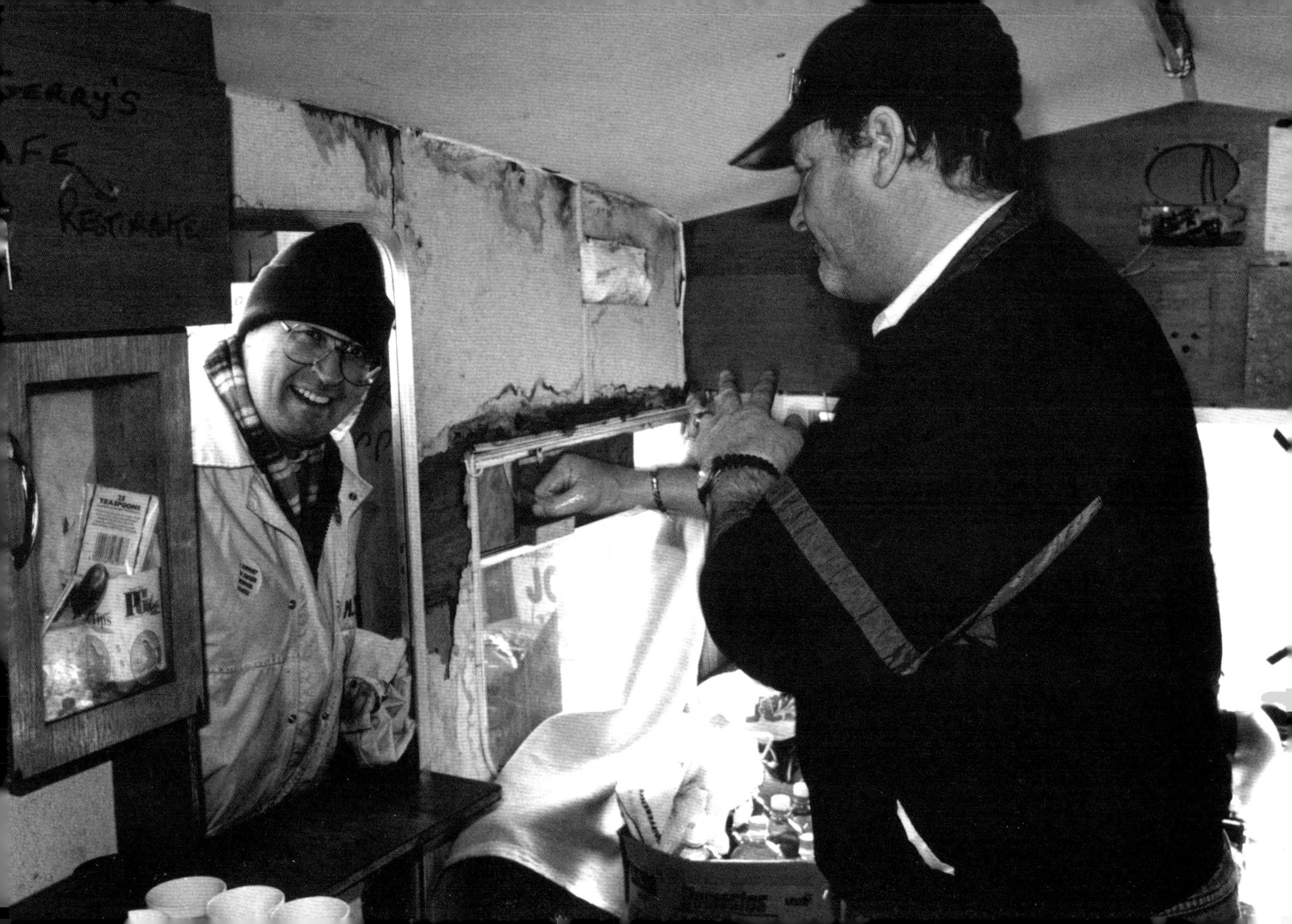

Above: MDHC block the Island where the Norse Irish picket took place, forcing the men across the road.

Left: The last picket.

Opposite: Sylvia at the very end, '98.

Overleaf left: One of the last pickets.

Overleaf right: Singing 'You'll Never Walk Alone' in the Dockers' Club at the end of the dispute.

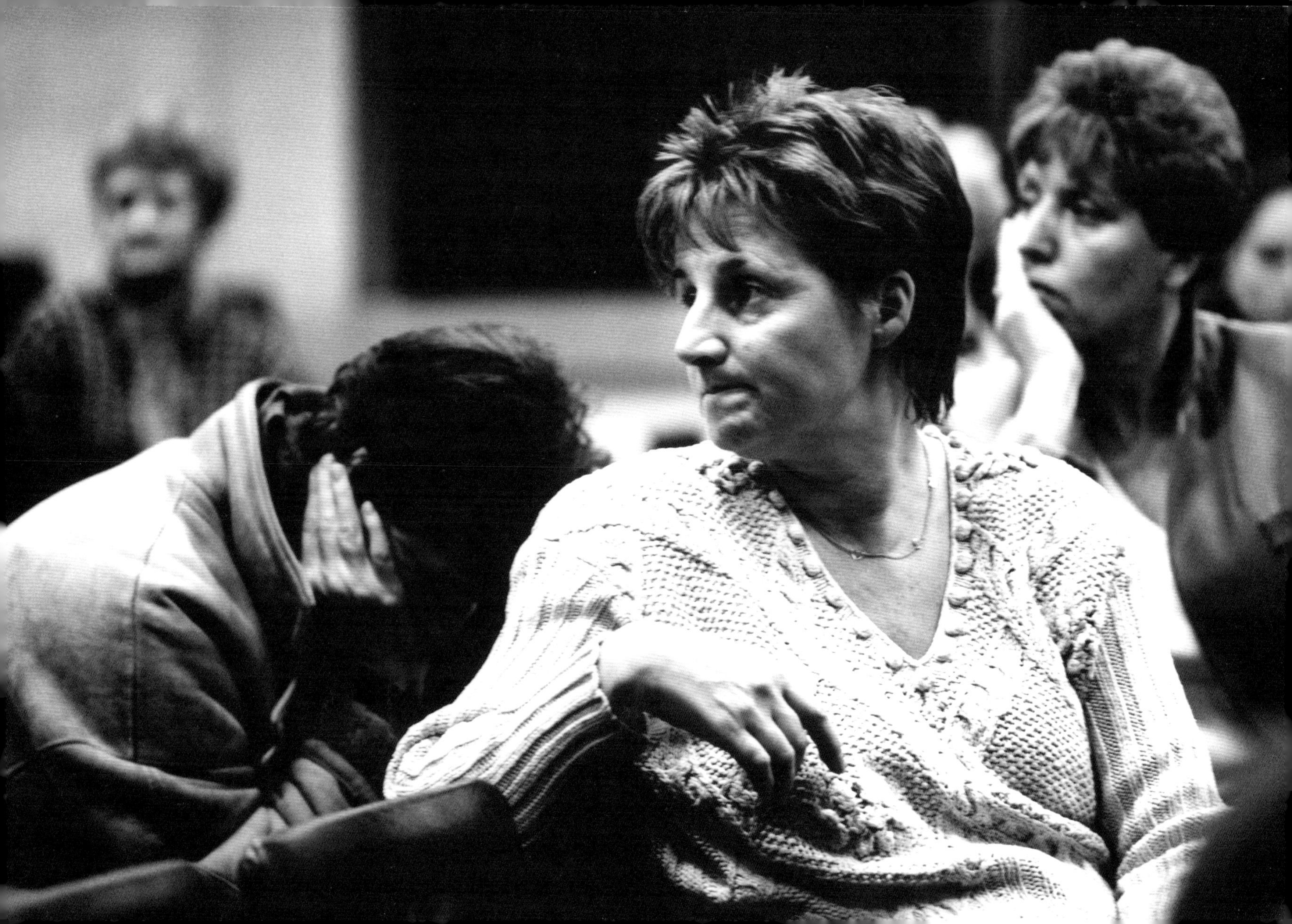

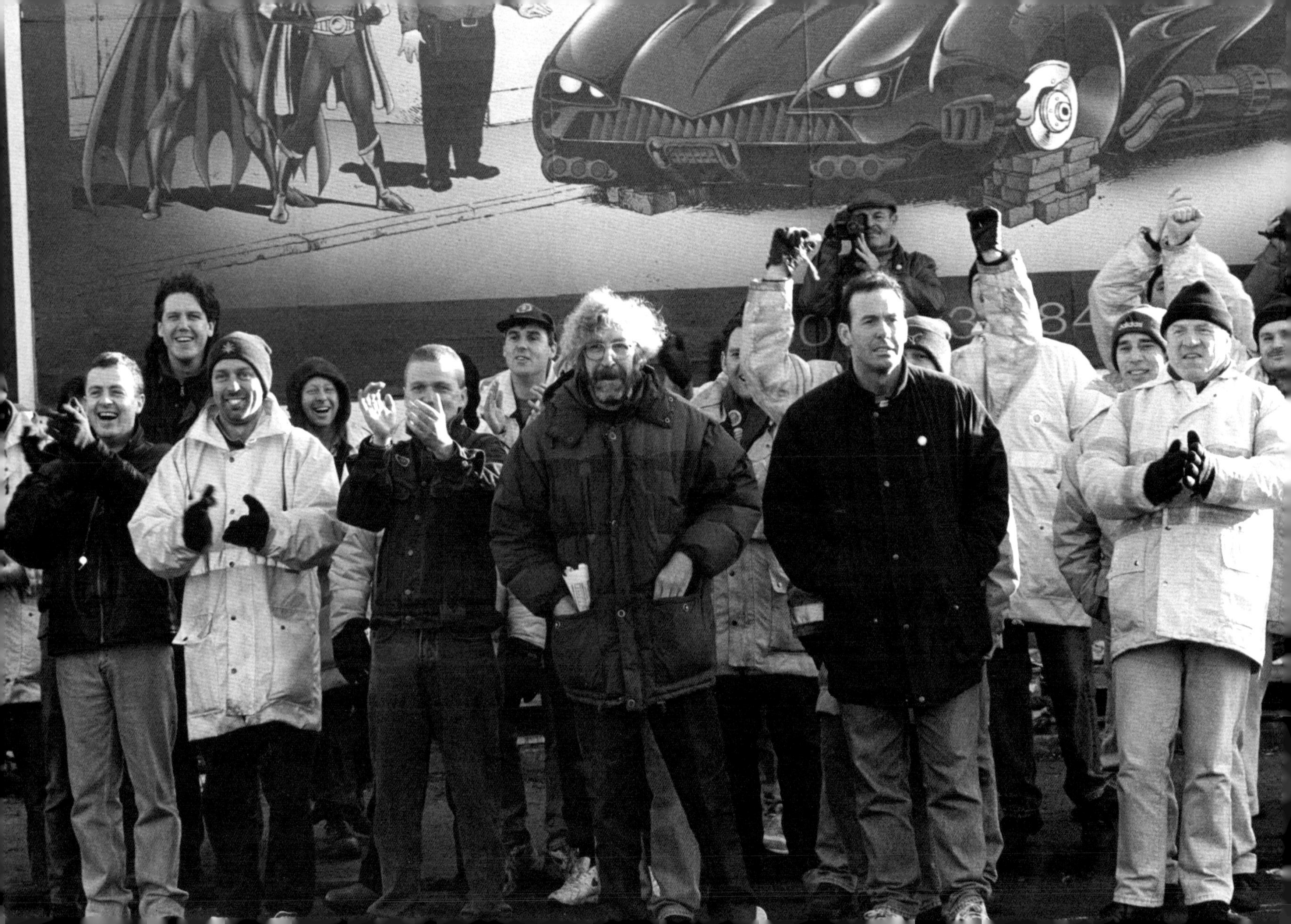

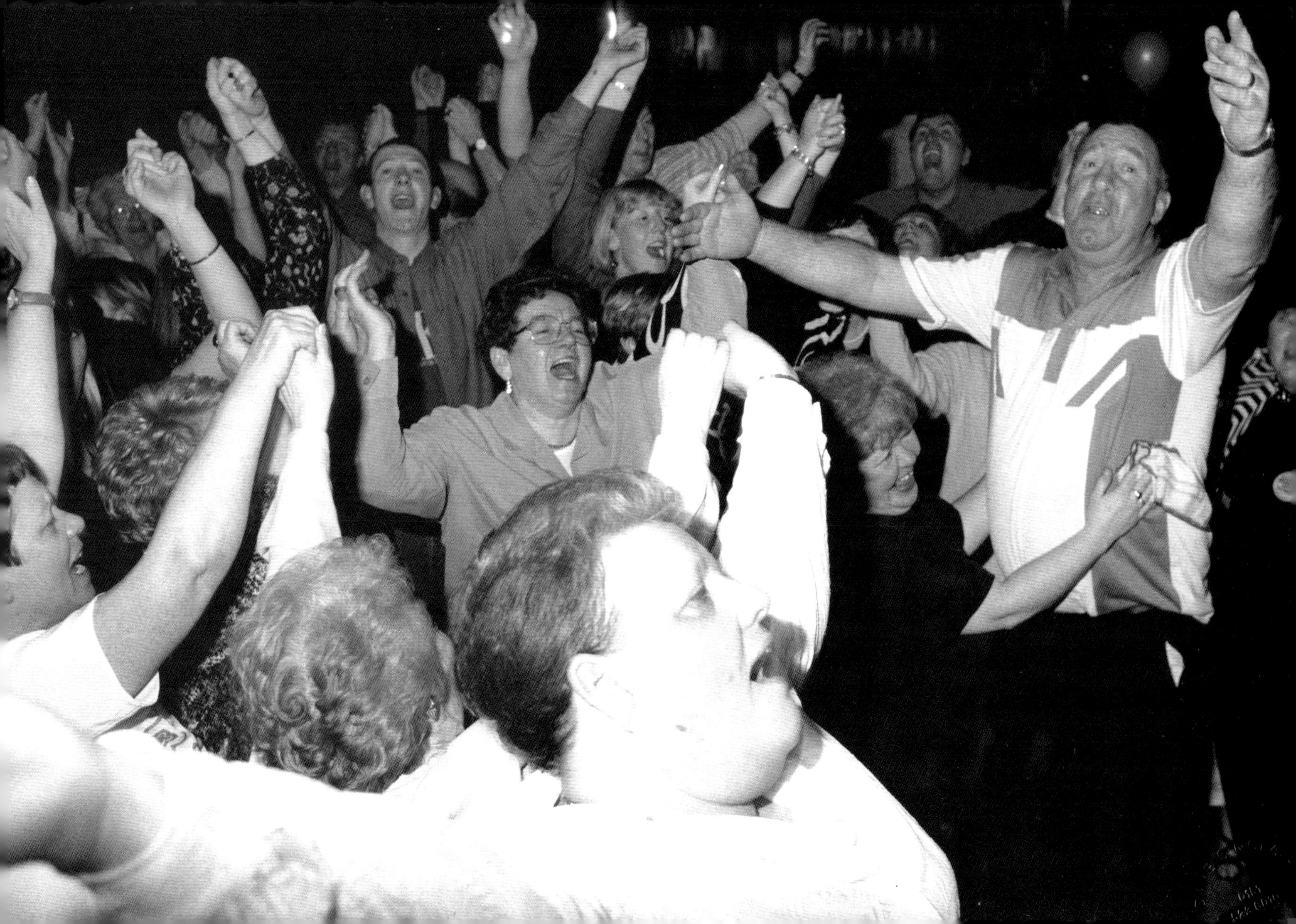

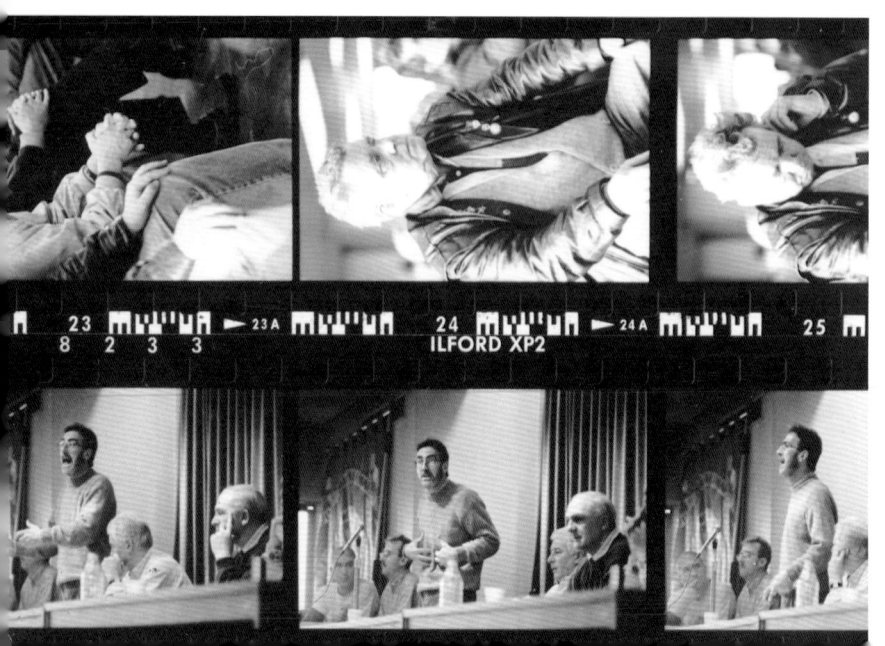

Above: Terry Woods on the last day, Feb '98.

Above left: Jimmy Nolan and Mike Carden after Snowy's funeral.

Below left: Mike Carden.

Opposite: Masher.

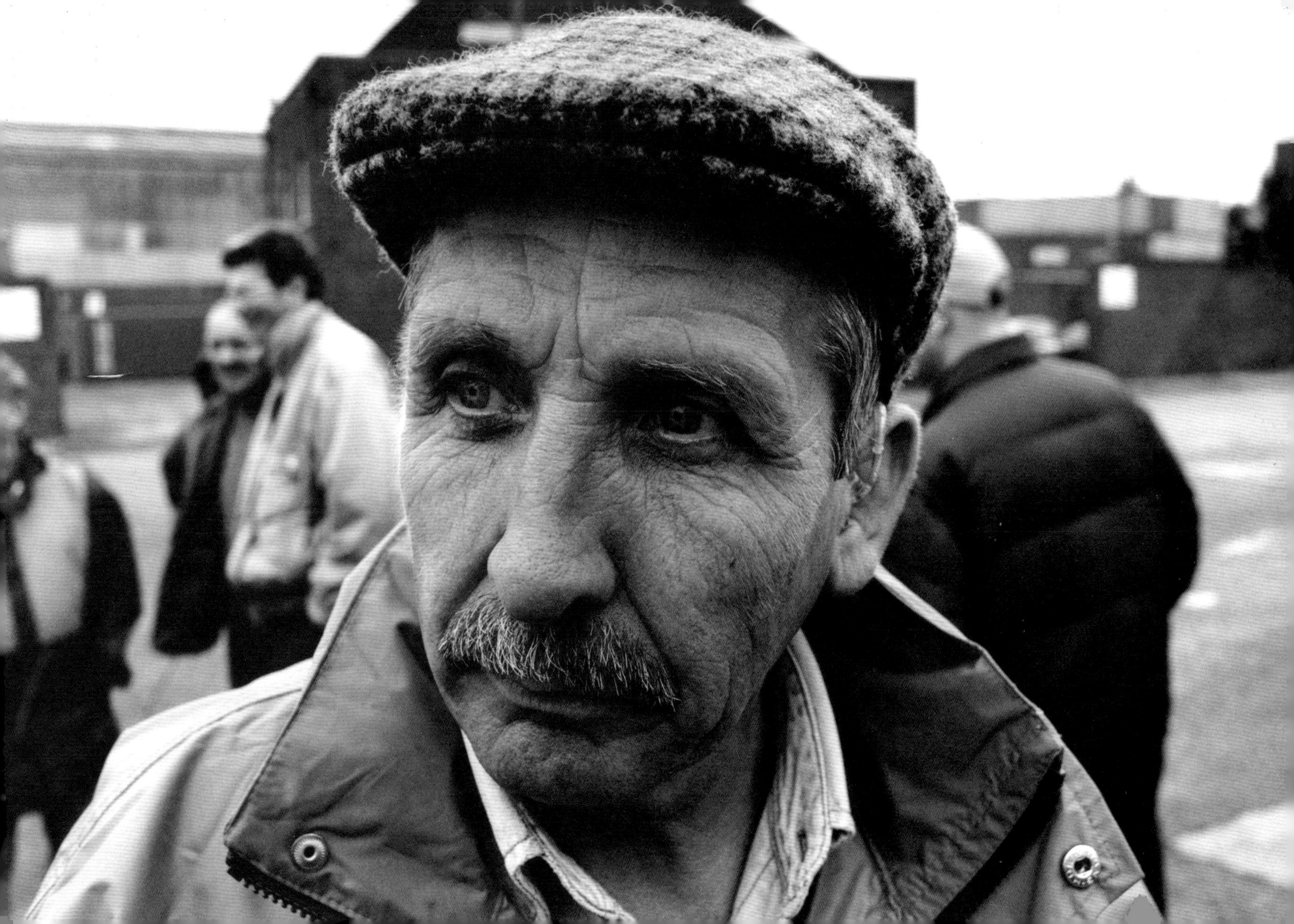

Joan, Val and Anne in the Lord Warden the afternoon the men voted to settle the dispute.

John Cowley, Tony Seasman, John Jackson, Jimmy Campbell and Eddie Leddon in Ma Edge's pub the afternoon the men voted to settle the dispute.

Dockers doing the 'Full Monty' in the Dockers' Club, Feb '98.

The wives watching.

The Liverpool dockers and their wives and families insist that theirs has been a very 'modern struggle, refuting the smug neo-liberal dismissal of dock labour as an atavistic throwback to an earlier mercantile age. Postmodernists, who fantasise a world of purely electronic and instantaneous contacts, blind to the slow movement of heavy necessary things, may indeed find this insistence on mere modernity quaint. (How *did* your tennis shoes get here from Indonesia, Mr and Mrs Jogger?) But against the pernicious idealist abstraction termed 'globalism', dockers enact an international solidarity based on intricate physical, intellectual, and above all social relationships to the flow of material goods. The dockers' line of contact extends outward from what is immediately at hand, to be lifted and stowed, and crosses the horizon to another space with similar immediacies. To sustain this solidarity, based on work, when work has been cravenly stolen away, is all the more admirable, sustaining hope for a future distinct from that fantasised by the engineers of a new world of wealth without workers. The dockers recognise this fantasy, and knowing full well that there can be no fully automated future, fathom its ugly secret motto: Everyone a Scab.

And ask Dave Sinclair to show his pictures, because he's been here in Liverpool all along the way, and has been thinking with his camera about the importance of the fence, and of grief.

Allan Sekula, Freeway to China (Version 2 for Liverpool), 2000.